Move!

Entering into God's Promises for You

Tim Hatch

Sermon To Book
www.sermontobook.com

Move! / Tim Hatch
ISBN-13: 978-1-952602-32-0

This book is the product of the amazing adventure of pastoring my first church for the past eighteen years. Waters Church has been my constant companion during my growing-up adult years. My wife, Cheryl, and I are privileged to work with wonderful people in New England who love Jesus and seek to make Him known. During our pastorate, we have shared our lives, our children's stories, our ups and downs with people who embody the phrase "salt of the earth." I know that there are many great churches in the world, but this place has been special.

While our movement as a church has been localized to the community we are in, the transition through the seasons has been both exciting and overwhelming at times. Each stage has helped us to discover more of God's power and grace. I dedicate this book to the church that showed me grace when I didn't really know what I was doing and the church that followed me when I started to have a better idea of what we should be.

We all need someone in our corner. My wife, Cheryl, Shane and Maryann Parsons, and Doug and Joannie White have been five of those people for me. No matter what challenges we faced, they stood strong in Christ for the mission. They believed when I couldn't and trusted me when it was scary.

To the friends who stayed with me in all of the moves God has brought us through, thank you and well done.

CONTENTS

Life Movement

In my second year of Bible college, I felt an overwhelming call to plant a church. But I had a problem: I was nineteen years old, and no one would give me that opportunity—rightfully so, if I'm honest. What God plants in our hearts is like a seed that needs a season of germination, watering, and patience before it sprouts from the earth.

Education for religious professionals teaches you a lot about Greek, Hebrew, Church history, and theology, but it doesn't teach you about life. That's a constant class in session for everyone, every day.

When I started out in vocational ministry as a youth pastor, I wanted to quit after only two weeks. I was ready to rethink my life and transition to something else. I remember vividly a conversation with my parents that helped me to press through that moment. The conversation was short, simple, and inspired by the Holy Spirit. I told them, "Mom and Dad, I've made a mistake. I need to quit."

They responded, "You're not moving back here, so you'd better give it another shot." I did, and the rest is my story.

I now know what I felt in that moment. It was that common sense of dread regarding the unknown. Life moves us forward, and we often chafe at the transitions to new chapters. After twenty-two years of vocational ministry, I have learned that the unknown is God's domain.

Over the past twenty years, I have had a front-row seat to the American Church in transition, and the ride I've been on could not have been anticipated. I grew up going to potlucks and youth revivals. Today I pastor a church in which hardly anyone knows what those are, and our regular worship resembles a concert. I remember when Sunday night service was for non-believers and Wednesday night Bible study was for believers who wanted to go deeper. Today neither exists in most churches. Many churches anticipate that most non-believers will attend a Sunday morning gathering.

The church I pastor has a story filled with movement, even though we've never moved very far geographically. In our first six years, we moved five times. We relaunched in 2010, and we have completely changed course on several large and small aspects of our church every step of the way. We learned to live with the mindset that "we can't stay here." Sometimes we lived it with joy, other times with vexation, but at all times by God's grace.

Change on the outside of the Church has also advanced rapidly. The world around the American Church has turned contentious in ways no one could have predicted. Today a business baking cakes for homosexual weddings is a line of demarcation in a culture war that could make enemies of those we are called to reach with the gospel of Christ, a gospel that saves all kinds of sinners. The coronavirus has rocked nations and aggravated our already contentious political divisions. The long-standing stain of racism has exposed many blind spots in American Christianity, and the results can be unsettling. The world is moving under our feet.

Sadly, the Church is no longer regarded as a sacred institution of American life. In many ways, she is being forced to the margins of society by an increasingly secular culture. Yet, through these transitions, I have seen our church make adjustments in the past and look forward to the changes in our future. We can embrace our current unknown for our good.

More than ever, Christians must learn to speak to the world in ways they will listen, but even those ways are changing constantly. What we did twenty years ago does not work anymore. What we do today will not work in the future. While the message of Jesus *never* changes, the method of delivery must. Engaging that change will determine whether your future will be better than your past.

I have vocational religious experiences to share, but this applies to all aspects of life. I started writing this book in 2019 and finished in 2020. I know that your industry and education today have already shifted radically in just a few months. I'm telling you what my parents told me decades ago: "You're not moving back here, so you'd better give it another shot." You have to adapt. You have to adjust. Growth and development are not just physical, inalterable realities; they are internal as well. Chances are good that you cannot eat or move the way you did twenty years ago or even twenty months ago.

This book is meant to help you navigate the inevitable transitions your life will make. Do you want some even more unnerving news? No one knows what tomorrow will bring in spite of all that yesterday presented. That's okay! Today is the day to embrace what showed up for you this morning and to let God move you through it.

We Can't Stay Here

Nothing brings as much anticipation as a vacation. It means time away from the kids, away from work, away from social media, email, and phone calls. We look forward to these trips, oftentimes counting down the days or mapping out what adventures we will take once we're there.

But then what happens? We arrive, we look around, we do a few things, and then we start looking forward to going home. "I'm ready to get back into my routine," we say. "I miss being home." The vacation ends, and we head home. Then what happens? "I should have enjoyed that time more! If only I could be on the beach again!"

We go on vacation because we can't stand being where we are. Then we get there, and it's not enough. We want to keep moving. We habitually want to be somewhere other than where we are. We want movement.

No matter where we are, no matter what we're doing, this desire to move calls to us. It's what we're used to. Your life has been moving from the moment you came into existence. Every action, every thought, every single thing that has happened to you—all have moved you to this very moment. Movement is inevitable. Change is inevitable. Whether you are an active participant or a passive bystander, your life will move, change, and evolve, with or without your consent.

As you read this book, depending upon where you are right now, you are sitting on a planet rotating at a speed of over 1,000 miles per hour while hurtling through space at 67,000 miles per hour and orbiting our sun in a solar system that is spinning around our galaxy at a rate of 490,000 miles per hour. And our galaxy is moving at about 1.3 million miles an hour![1]

Dizzy yet?

Above your head, the sun's rays are traveling 186,287 miles per second to shine down on your face,[2] and the clouds can move back and forth across the sky at a rate of 100 miles per hour.[3] Across the world, ocean tides ebb and flow, moving the 321,003,271 cubic miles of ocean back and forth twice a day.[4] Beneath your feet, Earth's core is spinning even faster than our planet rotates, and though we never notice it, the tectonic plates that cover the surface of the Earth move 1–2 inches per year.[5]

Right now, even if you sit very still, your body is constantly moving. Your lungs are expanding and contracting. Your heart will beat about 115,000 times today, pumping blood through 60,000 miles of blood vessels.[6]

Movement isn't only all around you; it's in you. And just as you move, so does time. This moment is here and gone, never to return. Did you miss it?

Life moves whether we want it to or not. The question

is: How do we respond? Do we float along, letting movement happen to us without intentional engagement? Do we hold tightly to things, people, moments, and seasons, hoping finally to find some form of lasting peace? Or do we move and change with life?

Adjust Regularly So You Can Advance Continually

I live in Patriots country. I ask for your forgiveness in advance if you do not live in New England. The church I get to pastor is minutes from Gillette Stadium, home of the most hated football team in the country. Love them or hate them, you can't deny their long and sustained success under Coach Bill Belichick. As the leader of a Christian church, I have gleaned many important leadership and life principles from their success. One of them is embracing, not avoiding, movement.

In their sixth championship run, a secret to their success was revealed in a program detailing their 2018 playoff campaign. The program explained that head coach Bill Belichick, the oldest and longest tenured (and most successful) coach in the league, adjusts his game plan based on what he has and what his team can do well at the moment.

Think about that. Instead of holding on to older methods or being stuck in a "this is how we've always done it" mindset, the Patriots seek opportunities to win however and wherever they can. If anyone could tell himself that his past success should dictate his present strategies, it's Bill Belichick. Yet for him and the entire organization, it's not about holding on to a previously successful script or repeating the same strategies that won yesterday's victories. A recent Forbes article highlighted their success in ten leadership principles, one of them being their willingness to change: "Belichick and Brady subscribe to the 'no one is paying us today for what we did yesterday' philosophy. The Patriots are always in the hunt."[7]

Success on the field of life is about moving, adapting, and never allowing this moment to freeze your spirit and your heart in time. You can't stay here.

What about when you lose? Belichick famously responded to a blow-out loss to the Chiefs in 2014 by answering every press member's question with, "We are on to Cincinnati." The press hated it, and fans didn't understand it, but his team loved it. They moved on from that terrible game and went on to win three more Super Bowls in five years. (Again, I apologize if you're not from New England.)

Life does not have a rewind button, so my question is this: Will you move forward intentionally? Will you move with gladness in your heart, knowing that your Father is looking out for you and offering help and guidance? Will you step into what He has for you?

Change that is directed by God and embraced by people who know that God is in the business of doing good things for His children is the very kind of change that will reinvent and reorganize your life. When this kind of change is active in your life, who you are today will not be who you are five years from now. This kind of change cannot be stopped so long as we are open to allowing God to move as only He can.

Although the world is changing at lightning speed, it seems that our willingness to change is one of the great lost arts of our current society. We love movement, but not when it means that we have to step outside of our comfort zone. We love opportunity, but not when it isn't clearly defined and guaranteed. We have forgotten what it is to dare to make a change, take that step, and enter into what could be.

This aversion to momentum has poisoned our churches and our Christianity. God offers opportunities and a better way, yet we wait, praying for something else, wanting something more comfortable, something easier, something safe. It's time that we rewrite the playbook. It's time we dare to trust that if we move with God, we will win every time.

The Opportunity of Obstacles

God's very first commandment was to move. He put Adam and Eve on this planet in Genesis 1:28 and basically said, "Now multiply and make babies and spread out." In other words, *move.*

Of course, we didn't stop there. Theologians call the first words of God to Adam and Eve the "Creation Mandate."[8] In other words, don't just move out, but advance with God's creation in diverse and interesting ways.

We've been doing that pretty well. We went from walking to riding horses to traveling by automobile, train, and airplane. Now we have companies trying to figure out how to move people to Mars!

Our need for change is so intrinsic to who we are that

it simply cannot be stopped. Will you move with God or without Him? Will you move toward God, or will you run? Will you move in the direction He has for you, or will you move in the direction of selfish ambition, personal desire, and self-seeking aspirations? You might not have considered this until now, but God *wants* you to move. You are part of that moving creation I talked about in the opening of this book. You are made to move. Thankfully, God wants to help us move with intention, purpose, and love. If we fail to move with Him, we will forfeit His best intentions for us. I would like to illustrate this with a parable.

The Blessing of the Billionaire

There is a story of a billionaire who decided that he wanted to make a difference in the world. He called his staff together and said, "How many orphans could I adopt financially? I'd pay for their food, clothing, housing, healthcare, and education through college. How many could I help?" The staff took a look at the billionaire's finances and came back with an astounding number. He had the resources to adopt 600,000 orphans financially.

The billionaire moved forward. He set up financial provisions for 600,000 orphans and put together a clear path to success. He told them, "Follow this path, and I will make sure that you succeed."

The orphans were overjoyed. Suddenly anything was possible! They got into school; they went to work. They moved into the blessing that the billionaire offered them. But as time wore on, their perspectives changed.

They doubted the billionaire's intentions. *He wants to control me!*

They doubted the path he set for them. *I know what's best for my life. He doesn't!*

They doubted his existence. *I've never seen him, so how could he possibly exist?*

The evidence of the billionaire's existence, love, and care were in the many blessings he had given the orphans, but it was no longer enough. All but two orphans decided to give up on the program. They couldn't take the tests, they hated the meal plan, and they scorned the living conditions. On top of that, they never came to terms with the fact that the rules were for their good. They fell off the path, giving in to drunkenness, promiscuity, and their passions. They dropped out of school and forfeited their future.

The two who stayed with it were able to complete the program successfully and go on to get their master's degrees. Their lives were changed forever. Not only this, but they also impacted the lives of billions more.

Sound familiar? The story is a parable of what we see in the Bible. God sent word to His 600,000 material orphans who had become enslaved to the nation of Egypt. He promised to meet their needs and lead them to freedom in a land of milk and honey. All they needed to do was to follow His plan. But of the 600,000 Israelites whom God delivered out of slavery in Egypt, only two, Joshua and Caleb, made it to the promised land of Canaan.

These two guys teach us how to move with God. They

proved that God is not just in the business of saving us from something that is bad for us. Rather, He wants to bring us into something that is good for us. He doesn't just want to get us to stop doing certain things; He wants us to embrace accomplishing great things. He wants to *move* us into our own personal promised land, a place where we not only experience His best for us, but also become vehicles of His blessing to those coming after us.

Here we begin our journey. We will spend the rest of this book taking a long look at Joshua and Caleb to find seven key values of moving with God. At the end of each chapter, a workbook section will help to motivate you to move with God in your own life. Your future depends on it! Your ten-year-older self will thank you for leaning in here and paying close attention. These stories are written, as Paul said, "for our instruction, that through endurance and through the encouragement of the Scriptures we might have hope" (Romans 15:4).

Let's get moving.

CHAPTER ONE

Movement Mindset #1— Be Opportunistic

So Joshua did as Moses told him, and fought with Amalek,
while Moses, Aaron, and Hur went up to the top of the hill.
—Exodus 17:10

How would you feel if you had spent your entire life as a slave and then someone asked you to lead a military campaign? Movement with God is often that fast. No one understood that better than Joshua. The first time his name appears in the Bible is in Exodus 17.

Then Amalek came and fought with Israel at Rephidim. So Moses said to Joshua, "Choose for us men, and go out and fight with Amalek. Tomorrow I will stand on the top of the hill with the staff of God in my hand." So Joshua did as Moses told him, and fought with Amalek, while Moses, Aaron, and Hur went up to the top of the hill. Whenever Moses held up his hand, Israel prevailed, and whenever he lowered his hand, Amalek prevailed. But Moses' hands grew weary, so they took a stone and put it under him, and he sat on it, while Aaron and Hur held up his hands, one on one side, and the other on the other side. So his hands were steady until the going down of the sun. And Joshua overwhelmed Amalek and his people with the sword.

Then the LORD said to Moses, "Write this as a memorial in a book and recite it in the ears of Joshua, that I will utterly blot out the memory of Amalek from under heaven." And Moses built an altar and called the name of it, The LORD Is My Banner, saying, "A hand upon the throne of the LORD! The LORD will have war with Amalek from generation to generation."

—Exodus 17:8–16

Before this passage, God brought the Israelites miraculously through the Red Sea (Exodus 14). The Egyptian army was in pursuit, and God parted the waters so that the people of Israel could walk across the sea on dry land. Pharaoh and his army followed and were washed away in the sea.

Before that, the Israelites had witnessed the ten plagues, ten powerful miracles from God Himself (Exodus 7–12). Later they would receive bread from heaven, water from a rock, and so much more (Exodus 16–17). The Bible shows how, time and again, things went from miraculous to perilous and back to miraculous. That's exactly how life goes, isn't it?

The billionaire always keeps his end of the bargain. As we move through life, God promises that while we can't stay *here*, He will help us to get *there*.

In this passage from Exodus, we see Joshua's first big moment. He might have hesitated, thinking, "I'm a former slave. I've never held a sword before! I've never fought in a war! How am I supposed to fight this guy?" But instead of letting fear and unfamiliarity prevent him from stepping into what God had for him, Joshua *moved*. He rose to the challenge and took advantage of the present opportunity, even when he had never done anything like this before. It was then that he saw God come through.

Don't Wait for Your Dreams

The heading of this section sounds like heresy in today's American culture. Every child seems to be constantly admonished to follow his or her dreams, to chase them and never let anyone get in the way. Sadly, this may exacerbate a problem for children who are told one thing during their key developmental stages and then experience another thing when real life kicks in.

The harsh reality of life is that no one else is really concerned about *your* dreams. The world is moving forward with or without you. While your dreams are part of you, they must not be the "god" of you. Following dreams instead of God's voice in the key turning points of your life may frustrate you. My advice is to let dreams be imaginations that inspire you, not decisions that advance you.

Joshua made it to the promised land, but it wasn't easy. He wandered with his people, took on a role as a spy, and had to fight battle after battle to enter into what God had promised him, yet he continued to move. He saw obstacles as opportunities.

If we're going to move with God, we need to view life in the same way. God may allow problems and setbacks, things that are completely overwhelming, and we have two choices. We can go our own way, or we can view those obstacles as opportunities. When difficulties come, we can believe either that God has let us down or that God has set us up for a victory. We can move away from His promises or into them.

There is nothing that comes into your life that has not been Father-filtered. God knows the beginning and the end. There may be a fight, but my Bible tells me in Isaiah that no weapon formed against me is going to prevail (Isaiah 54:17 NIV). If we read a bit further, we find that *"this* is the *heritage* of the servants of the LORD" (Isaiah 54:17 NIV, emphasis added).

Heritage is where you come from. It's your background. It's the history, the people, and the circumstances that have led up to your existence and this very moment. For some of us, heritage is an excuse for how and who we are. We look at our upbringing and our disadvantages and hurts, and we use those things to explain why we're angry, jealous, or unsuccessful. But the Bible says that if we're in Christ, we have a new heritage. This new heritage offers protection and assurance, no matter what. It's ours to grab hold of, even though we've done nothing to deserve it—that's grace!

We live in a world infatuated with the concept of karma. We think, "If I do good, life will give me good. If someone does me wrong, life will get that person back." I say this respectfully, but karma is completely unbiblical. God does not operate according to karma. He operates according to grace, and grace is undeserved.

It's not your goodness that makes things go well for you. It's not your works or reputation. It's God's righteousness given to us when we believe Him. At the moment of salvation, Jesus takes charge of our lives and begins to move us in His direction. When that happens, He takes ownership of both our good and our bad and begins to work them out for His purposes.

Moving with God, therefore, means moving by His grace and not by our works or actions. It means accepting His love and the heritage that He has for us. Then we begin to see how the obstacles before us are not punishments for bad things we've done or ways we've fallen off track. They are opportunities to move further into our heritage and God's grace. Obstacles are opportunities for blessing, but we need to take them as they come.

Take What You're Given

God sends us opportunities, but often they aren't the ones we want or dream about. We can struggle with this. Especially when we're young, this can be hard to accept because we may look at the success of older people who seem to love their lives and assume that they got exactly what they wanted all along the way. I can assure you that rarely happens for anyone.

Our current culture has sold us a bad bill of goods in regard to our dreams. We have been told ad nauseam to follow our dreams and chase our passions, but what happens when God begins to move us in a different direction? What happens when we find ourselves surrounded by people we don't like, doing a job we'd rather quit, and we receive no recognition for it?

Moving with God means accepting the fact that no, you can't be whatever *you* want. You can't fulfill *your* dreams.

You don't have the power to define your own existence. And when the going gets rough, there's no such thing as a "safe space" in the real world.

Rather, you must understand that you are accountable to a holy and righteous God. He decides where you go and what you become. He provides the safety and comfort you need. And through Him, your wildest dreams and greatest passions will seem insignificant. Think of that!

I love Mike Rowe, the host of *Dirty Jobs*, who travels the world introducing us to people employed at doing things no one dreams about. He once said, "The people I've met on my journeys, by and large, didn't set out to realize their dream. They looked around for an opportunity. They identified the opportunity. They exploited the opportunity. They worked at the opportunity. Then they got good at the opportunity. Then they figured out how to love it."[9]

A life spent moving forward with Christ isn't about waiting for the perfect opportunity. It's about taking the one that's right in front of you. I guarantee you that there's an opportunity staring you in the face at this very moment. You may not see it. It's hiding behind the fog of your dreams.

My dream was to start a church. I went to college to learn how to study the Bible and be a pastor. Near graduation, I sent out résumé after résumé. I was desperate for a church and wanted to avoid the shame of moving in with my parents. I only got two responses. One was from a church in Pittsburgh. This church made it clear that they had a very large pool of candidates and experience was a priority for them. The likelihood of me getting the position was next to nothing. The other church that responded called me one day and asked if I'd be interested in part-time youth ministry.

Youth ministry? Part time? That was far from my dream. I imagined that Bible education entitled me to be an excellent associate or perhaps even lead pastor of a smaller (much more desperate) church, not a part-time youth minister! On top of that, I had only taken one youth ministry course through college. On top of that, I didn't even like teenagers! I started to wrestle in prayer with this choice: "What is my purpose? What is my calling? What are my gifts, Lord? Where do You want me?!"

I spent a lot of time searching when the opportunity was right in front of me. I remember my roommate, Damien, coming to me one day and saying, "Why are you praying about where to go, Tim? You only have one offer on the table!"

I couldn't argue with him. I knew that he was right. I accepted the youth ministry position, and two weeks in, I was in trouble. The kids hated me and didn't listen to me, and I found out through the grapevine that they actually planned to haze me! *Haze me? They want to haze their shepherd? Are these kids even Christian? Get me out of here!*

Recall the conversation with my parents I mentioned earlier: "You aren't moving back here, so you'd better give it another shot." Thank God for parents who can speak truth to their children when they don't want to hear it. I dug down deep and put in my best effort for youth ministry that next year. Then one year became two years, which became six years. I started youth ministry hating teenagers, and by the time I was finished in that position, I had tears rolling down my face during my last night as their pastor.

This opportunity that I did not want eventually led me to the opportunity I desired. The church's pastor, Thomas Geyser, who is my mentor and had become my father-in-law during that time, brought me into his office one day and said the following words: "We're starting a church in an area south of us. Would you like to be the pastor of that church?" Finally, my "dream" opportunity presented itself: church planter and lead pastor! But it was on the other side of an opportunity that I scorned and almost rejected.

Christ taught this principle in the Gospels. He said, "One who is faithful in a very little is also faithful in much" (Luke 16:10). Maybe it's time for you to look at the opportunity you don't want and see it for what it is: a test of your character. Will you do your best even in something that isn't in your dreams? There's great opportunity awaiting you on the other side of what you may not want to do.

If we wait for things to move in the direction *we* want, we'll be waiting forever. But when we step forward into the opportunities in front of us, God continues to move us. Doors open when we put our heads down and do the work. Things happen when we trust God and bravely enter into what He has for us.

Remember Your Intercessor

All this talk about taking undesired opportunities may have you feeling anxious about the next stage of life. I'm sure that Joshua was shaking in his shoes when Moses first brought this opportunity to him. Thankfully, Joshua was told very clearly that he would not be fighting alone. Moses was going to be on the mountain, praying for him and the army. Now, if I had the choice of anyone from history praying for me, Moses would be in the top three on my list. While Joshua might have felt the weight of responsibility in taking on Amalek, he had the comfort of knowing that Moses was interceding for him.

The story of Joshua fighting the Amalekites gives us further counsel when we look at what Moses did in that situation. As Joshua fought, Moses lifted his hands to God on behalf of Israel's army. This is a picture we must remember if we are going to move forward with confidence.

So Joshua did as Moses told him, and fought with Amalek, while Moses, Aaron, and Hur went up to the top of the hill. Whenever Moses held up his hand, Israel prevailed, and whenever he lowered his hand, Amalek prevailed.
—Exodus 17:10–11

People who move with God will tell you that they aren't operating in their own strength. They aren't alone in the process. Every person who is stepping into the God-ordained opportunities in front of him or her is backed by a support system of intercessors.

An intercessor is somebody who prays for you. These

people go to the throne daily and ask God for clarity in your life. They pray over your situations and your fears. They ask for wisdom and direction, and they are an incredible blessing.

You may not have anyone in your life who can fill this role. Perhaps you are new to the faith, new to a church, or in a position in which fellowship with other believers is limited. Know this: Jesus is your intercessor.

> *Since then we have a great high priest who has passed through the heavens, Jesus, the Son of God, let us hold fast our confession.*
> **—Hebrews 4:14**

Exodus 17:12 says that Aaron and Hur held up the arms of Moses when they grew tired. They also gave him a rock to sit on while he stayed on that mountain in prayer for Joshua's victory. I have this image of Moses growing tired, with his knees bent and his outstretched arms being held by Aaron and Hur on each side of him. When I picture this scene with Moses in that posture, I see the very same posture of Christ when He hung on the cross, tired from carrying it to Golgotha, yet fixed in place on the right and left by the nails.

Jesus is our true Moses. He made the necessary blood sacrifice for you and me to enter into the presence of God and make our requests known to our Father, thus securing peace that our minds cannot fully comprehend (Philippians 4:7). What a promise we have through the work of Jesus Christ for us! You may feel overwhelmed in a new venture or a job that you think is a dead end. I want you to see it as God's appointed opportunity for you. He is making it possible for you to succeed in that place. You may hate it at first, as I did, but you need to see it as God's training academy to develop skills that will stay with you as you climb to new and extraordinary heights. In Christ Jesus, you have the support you need to make the most of this moment. You are where you are on purpose, and better things are in your future. It's time for you to view your obstacles as opportunities and Jesus as your number-one support system.

WORKBOOK

Chapter One Questions

Question: What are some opportunities in your life right now? How are these different from your dreams for your life? What obstacles are in your way, and how may each of these present a hidden opportunity?

_____

_____

_____

_____

_____

_____

_____

_____

_____

_____

Question: Do you operate on the principle of karma or the promise of grace? How does your mindset concerning karma compared to grace affect your decisions and your view of your past, present, and future? How can you track God's grace through your heritage?

_____

_____

_____

_____

_____

_____

_____

_____

_____

_____

_____

_____

Journal: *If we wait for things to move in the direction we want, we'll be waiting forever. But when we step forward into the opportunities in front of us, God continues to move us.* What is an opportunity before you on which you don't want to act? What is holding you back? Do you feel unqualified, unworthy, or uninterested? Go to Jesus, your intercessor, and ask for His help, guidance, strength, and support for the opportunity you need to accept and undertake.

_____

_____

_____

_____

_____

_____

_____

_____

_____

_____

Action: Talk to an older person who has been able to build a dream career, a dynamic family, or a thriving ministry. Ask this person to share some of the experiences he or she had when first moving forward with God. How did this person take the opportunities presented to him or her, and how did those first steps of obedience grow into greater opportunities?

Chapter One Notes

_____

_____

_____

_____

_____

_____

_____

_____

_____

_____

_____

_____

_____

_____

_____

_____

_____

_____

CHAPTER TWO

Movement Mindset #2— Be Properly Dissatisfied

Thus the LORD used to speak to Moses face to face, as a man speaks to his friend. When Moses turned again into the camp, his assistant Joshua the son of Nun, a young man, would not depart from the tent.
—***Exodus 33:11*** *(emphasis added)*

When we study the life of Joshua historically, we make a big mistake. We begin with Joshua 1:1.

It makes sense. We want to learn about Joshua, so we go to the beginning of his book, assuming that we're in the right place. Joshua 1:1 is the moment when the baton was taken from Moses and given to Joshua. It was the official start of Joshua's ministry as leader of the Israelites. But that is not when Joshua's story began. God was speaking to him and preparing him even before that point in time.

God spoke words of encouragement to Joshua that still resonate with generations today. If you take a moment to read Joshua 1, you will see how much empowerment God spoke into Joshua's life. Joshua then took the encouragement he heard from God and conquered the enemy in every direction.

Make no mistake. Joshua didn't wake up one day and suddenly have this close relationship with God and the opportunity to lead. It's not like he could suddenly hear God the moment Moses disappeared. This moment came after many, many years of Joshua developing a relationship with God. That's why we can't simply start at Joshua 1:1.

Moses was one of the greatest of God's leaders, and Joshua sat at his feet for four decades. That's forty years of learning, forty years of listening and watching, forty years of taking instruction from a man who walked and talked with God, forty years of *moving*. Imagine how Joshua must have felt upon Moses' death. His mentor was gone. It was just Joshua and God from there on out, and that must have been an intimidating thing. It's easy to start the story here, but we miss so much when we do that. You see, leading up to this incredible moment, leading up to the official start of Joshua's ministry, he had developed a proper dissatisfaction.

You Are Made to Crave

Human beings are, by nature, unsatisfied. This is why people sin. They think there are pleasures out there that will satisfy. They think there are things out there that will bring fulfillment. They chase food or drugs, pleasures in relationships, anything and everything to try to fill the void. We are cravers by nature.

I've seen a tendency in people to think that they need more in order to be considered wealthy. For example, someone making $50,000 a year thinks that if he were to make $75,000 a year, then he would be wealthy. However, the people making $75,000 a year often believe that $100,000 would make them wealthy. Those who make $100,000 claim to need $125,000, and on and on and on it goes. Even millionaires want more, thinking that an increase in money will bring an increase in contentment and happiness.

We are unsatisfied by nature! Is that bad? Not at all. I believe that we have this nagging dissatisfaction as a gift from God. It points us back to Him. In the garden of Eden, Adam and his wife had fulfillment and satisfaction in God, but they sinned and broke fellowship with Him. That broken fellowship exists in all of us, lurking daily in our hearts as a sense of something lost. No relationship, no job, no opportunity, no event, no feeling is going to bring the level of satisfaction that we crave. The *only* thing that can fill that void is God Himself.

One of my favorite quotes is from *The Weight of Glory* by C. S. Lewis.[10] It basically says that if we think about all that Jesus promises will happen for us if we follow Him, it seems that our Lord finds our desires not too strong, but rather too weak. It's not the fact that we want something that is the problem. The problem is that our want is misdirected. According to Lewis—and I would agree with him—God offers something far better than what you and I think we want.

It's good that we are dissatisfied because that dissatisfaction points us to God. Joshua caught this. He watched

Moses walk with God. Imagine Joshua hearing Moses tell the story of meeting God in the burning bush and something catching fire in his own heart. Why else would he go all the way from Egypt to the promised land? Why else would he follow Moses so closely and listen to God's commands so wholeheartedly? He wanted what Moses had. He knew that life with God was the best gift he could receive, and he wanted nothing more than to have it.

What If You Could Have a Good Life Without God?

In Exodus 32, the Israelites made a golden calf, worshiped it, and sacrificed to it. They prostituted themselves to this statue, and Moses was ticked. He had just come down from the mountain where he had received the Ten Commandments. He smashed the commandment tablets, and just like that, thousands were struck down. A plague and judgment came from the heavens. God had had enough.

In Exodus 33:1–3, God made a new offer to Israel. He would still give them the land, the blessing, and the riches that He had always intended to give them, but He would not be with them. Think about getting everything you want but having none of God's presence. I think that a lot of Americans today would say, "Sign me up!" But the Israelites understood the depth of the situation. They understood that a day when God was offering them everything apart from Himself was a day of disaster.

Exodus 33:4 reads, "When the people heard this disastrous word, they mourned, and no one put on his ornaments." They had taken off their ornaments to worship the idol, and here they were, refusing to put them back on. Their position was clear: "We are done with the old ways; we only want God."

This is the dissatisfaction you need and want, a dissatisfaction with the good life without God. This dissatisfaction can move us where God is going. It can move us toward the presence of God. This kind of dissatisfaction is what motivates us to improve our churches, our marriages, and our homes. It's what pushes us into presence with the King. It has nothing to do with chasing after a bigger salary, a larger congregation, or a fatter bank account. It has to do with the inner fulfillment that cannot be found apart from Him.

Augustine was a church father around 400 AD. He was born to a Christian mother and a pagan father.[11] His whole life, Augustine's mother prayed for him to know Christ. At first, Augustine rejected this. He wanted to have fun. He wanted to choose his passions and chase his lust and desires. He was a womanizer. He was an alcoholic. He went through all the things that average, ordinary human beings go through when they're searching. He pursued all the pleasures he could find, and he found that they were empty. He found that they were hollow. He found no rest for his anxious soul.

One day, Augustine prayed for direction in his directionless life. On the table was his mother's Bible. He opened it and came to Romans 13, which reads:

The night is far gone; the day is at hand. So then let us cast off the works of darkness and put on the armor of light. Let us walk properly as in the daytime, not in orgies and drunkenness, not in sexual immorality and sensuality, not in quarreling and jealousy. But put on the Lord Jesus Christ, and make no provision for the flesh, to gratify its desires.

—Romans 13:12-14

Augustine would go on to share that when he read those words, the love of God burst into his heart, and all the passions of the flesh were gone. He found the satisfaction he was searching for in God.

Augustine became one of the great defenders of the Church. To this day, he is quoted around the world by pastors and Christian leaders. One of his most notable sayings is this: "Thou has made us for thyself and our heart is restless until it finds its rest in thee."[12] Augustine knew the feeling of nagging dissatisfaction well; it's what drove him to the throne of Jesus. He recognized that particular dissatisfaction as a gift from God.

Head into the Tent

After coming down from the mountain and dealing with the people's idolatry and repentance, Moses needed some time away. He set up a tent to meet with God (Exodus 33:7). He needed a quiet, secluded space where he could deal with everything that was going on around him. He called it a tent of meeting, and he opened it up to anyone who wanted to seek the Lord.

Spending time with God is a good practice for anyone

dealing with dissatisfaction. When your business is going crazy, when life is going nuts, when your marriage is on the fritz, when you can't stand your kids anymore, get away! Create a private place where it's just you and God. That's what Moses did, and here's what happened:

> *Whenever Moses went out to the tent, all the people would rise up, and each would stand at his tent door, and watch Moses until he had gone into the tent. When Moses entered the tent, the pillar of cloud would descend and stand at the entrance of the tent, and the LORD would speak with Moses. And when all the people saw the pillar of cloud standing at the entrance of the tent, all the people would rise up and worship, each at his tent door.*
> *—Exodus 33:8–10*

I find it interesting that so many people would watch Moses go into the tent. They would stand at the door and admire what he was doing, but they wouldn't go into the tent themselves. Think about that. These people were content to associate with and admire a spiritual person. They weren't necessarily willing to dive in themselves.

This is what made Joshua different. The Bible says that when Moses left the tent, Joshua stayed. He remained waiting at the tent, eager to be present the next time Moses entered. Joshua wanted to be part of what was going on; he didn't want merely to watch and celebrate like the rest.

> *Thus the LORD used to speak to Moses face to face, as a man speaks to his friend. When Moses turned again into the camp, his assistant Joshua the son of Nun, a young man, would not depart from the tent.*
> *—Exodus 33:11*

God wants you to move into the tent. He wants to have a direct personal relationship with you, not a relationship by association, not a relationship through your pastor or your mentor or your religious rituals. He wants you to spend time in His presence, experiencing His power, so that you can move forward on purpose.

The reason we need to spend time in the tent with God is simple: a lot of things are taught, but most things are caught. You can go to church for a long time, and then suddenly the lights go on, and you *get it*. You're changed. You can pray over an issue in your life for years, and then one day, in an instant, you get the right word or direction from God to lead you out. You spend time with your Father, and you walk out the door with a completely different view of the world.

This book is the result of my personal decision to prioritize a "tent time" with God in my own life. In 2013, after spending years simply reading through the Bible every year for my personal devotions, I felt the Lord leading me to slow down, read one book of the Bible intensely for the whole year, and journal about my findings regularly. I got to Exodus 17 and started reading about Joshua, and my alone time with God became a powerful preaching series for our church while we worked hard to move into a brand-new facility. Now that series has become this book for you. You never know what will come out when you go into the tent with God.

You have to make this decision for yourself. Too many Christians are content with a third-party connection to God. When trouble hits, we pick up the phone and call a friend instead of heading into the tent. We look for outside validation instead of heading into the tent. We seek direction from mentors instead of heading into the tent. We check off all the church activities, but we don't head into the tent.

I've spent a lot of time with pastors who often forget that leading God's people has to be done by a person intimately familiar with God's presence. A man can preach, lead, and build a church, but if he has not been with God to deliver His Word according to His heart, what does he actually leave behind? All those other activities are fine, but tent time is the best time. Joshua understood this, and it catapulted him forward. It's been written down so that we will do the same. It's time to become unsatisfied with your status as a bystander. Become unsatisfied with a third-party connection to God. It's time to move into the tent.

Moving into God's Presence

As far as we know, Joshua didn't come from a line of perfect Jews. The Bible says that he was the son of Nun, but we don't know anything beyond that or even who Nun was and what he contributed to Israel's journey. Joshua was like most of us. We come from all kinds of backgrounds, some Christian, some pagan, and some in between. God doesn't work through natural bloodlines; He works through the supernatural bloodline of His Son, Jesus Christ.

Joshua moved forward despite not having the credentials one would expect. He was young, but he was willing. He was unsatisfied with a third-party connection to God.

Some people hear this challenge to move into the tent and assume that it's for other people, those who can't get their lives together. They think that going into the tent is a sign of weakness. They think that it's a sign of someone who doesn't have it all together. But Joshua was not weak. Joshua was a fighter. He was a commander of soldiers. He was the general of the army of the nation of Israel, and he hardly ever lost a battle. This strong, capable warrior knew that he needed to spend time in the tent and gain strength from God.

I say this because one of the most famous lies about Christianity is that it's for people who can't get their lives together. While that is theologically true, it's also true that no one really has his or her life completely together. We can all benefit from more time with God. Time in the tent is for both those far from God and those who already have their lives somewhat together (like Joshua) because we all need God's strength if we are going to move with God. There's a psalm that reads, "Blessed are those who dwell in your house, ever singing your praise!" (Psalm 84:4). Later in that passage, it reads, "They go from strength to strength…" (Psalm 84:7).

I think of Elijah, who stopped the rain from falling on the land for over three years (1 Kings 17, James 5:17). In our study of this story, we usually focus on the moment when he confronted the prophets of Baal on Mount Carmel (1 Kings 18:20–40). But the real story of Elijah is how fervently he prayed for God to work in Israel so that they might come back to Him. Elijah prayed that it would not rain in Israel. Why would he pray that his largely agrarian country would not see rain? Because Elijah knew the

Word of God. He understood that his nation was in rebellion toward the Lord and that judgment needed to happen to awaken their hearts and turn them back to Him. His prayers were inspired by Deuteronomy 28, where the Torah stipulates that a lack of rain would be a sign of God's curse for Israel's continued rebellion.

What do you think was happening in Elijah's life during this time of prayer? He was growing stronger in God. In fact, he got so strong that he was able to confront Ahab with holy boldness in spite of the associated risk. He shook a nation awake and turned them back to God because he practiced "tent time" himself. You can never lose when you set yourself apart to dwell with God. Joshua did not become Joshua simply because he did what Moses told him. Joshua became Joshua because he followed Moses' practice of spending time in the presence of God.

As I said in the introduction, my church moved six times in its first five years of existence. I remember when we got a building that looked like a church in our second year as a church. I felt like we had arrived. It sat less than 200 people, and though we had two services each weekend, God had a much bigger agenda in mind. It was a "tent moment" with God that launched a campaign for something much larger than and different from what we had anticipated.

I spent many afternoons walking through our sanctuary, praying for our church and its future. One particularly lovely day in New England, I flipped through my Bible, and the words of Isaiah 54 leaped off the page:

Enlarge the place of your tent, and let the curtains of your habitations be stretched out; do not hold back; lengthen your cords and strengthen your stakes. For you will spread abroad to the right and to the left, and your offspring will possess the nations and will people the desolate cities.
—Isaiah 54:2–3

It was one of those moments when I felt as though God wrote something in the Bible just for me. I knew immediately that there was no way we could stay in the building we had. Even though we were under contract to buy it, we backed out, and we lost tens of thousands of dollars. Then we leased (yes, *leased*) a space large enough to hold many more people. Who would have thought that my personal tent time would have impacted the tent of our church? Looking back, I can see how it all came together.

Time and again, God's Word leads us to move on to greater ventures and bigger opportunities. Yes, there will be challenges—and there were many with that particular transition for our church—but God was faithful every step of the way.

Some people think that the Bible is a bunch of rules intended to limit their enjoyment of life. Nonsense! The Bible is God's Word to empower your life. Are there proper boundaries to help us move in the right way? Yes, but they are all for our good. We never know what good we may be missing out on when we miss out on time in the tent with God.

I am who I am because of the power of God. I have moved into the tent with Him, and my life is vastly different. He has something for you, too. He has directions and a plan. He has prosperity, blessings, and success, and your first step is to go into that tent! Joshua is evidence of the incredible change that can occur if you make this decision to move.

> Have I not commanded you? Be strong and courageous. Do not be frightened, and do not be dismayed, for the LORD your God is **with you wherever you go**."
>
> —*Joshua 1:9* (emphasis added)

Joshua had spent years following Moses and learning from him the value of going into that tent. Even when Moses wasn't in the tent, Joshua stayed. He did this because he knew that he had to develop an ear to hear God's voice and live in God's presence. Joshua had taken steps to develop his own relationship with God and was, therefore, ready for the move. He brought all of this into what we read in Joshua 1. He was ready to move into the promised land in Joshua 1 simply based on God's promise when God told him, "You're going to be successful, and I am going to be with you every step of the way."

Let's Go Camping

Dissatisfaction causes us to search, and the more we search, the more we find that true satisfaction can only be found in God. Joshua grabbed hold of this. He dared to go into the tent when the rest of his friends and nation stayed outside, and his life was forever changed.

This isn't just for Joshua or for the super-spiritual or for pastors and leaders. This is for you. The Bible teaches that because of Jesus' work, we have access to God's presence.

> *Since then we have a great high priest who has passed through the heavens, Jesus, the Son of God, let us hold fast our confession. ... Let us then with confidence draw near to the throne of grace, that we may receive mercy and find grace to help in time of need.*
> **—Hebrews 4:14, 16**

Perhaps you've been let down in a search that was detached from your Father. Maybe you were scorned in love or laid off from work. Perhaps you got many of the things you aimed for and found out they weren't all that. Or maybe you just have that deep restlessness Augustine talked about 1,600 years ago. The question is: What are you going to do with that ache? Let your dissatisfaction lead you into a quiet place with God. Spend time there. Ask questions. Listen. And come out claiming the promises that God gave to Joshua. God's presence will empower the movement of your life if only you will make that first move of going into the tent.

WORKBOOK

Chapter Two Questions

Question: List some areas of your life with which you are dissatisfied, naming the first things that come to mind. Does your list show a preoccupation with trivial and worldly things, or does it show a craving for God and His best? What do you long for, and how does each of these longings ultimately point back to something only God can fulfill?

_____

_____

_____

_____

_____

_____

_____

_____

Question: Give an example of someone you know (or know of) who is living "the good life" apart from God. Do you think that he or she is ultimately satisfied? If yes, do you think that this person's satisfaction will last and sustain him or her through the inevitable difficulties of life? Why or why not? Contrast this life with someone who has been persecuted for following Christ. Is it possible to be satisfied with a very difficult life?

Journal: Who has been a spiritual mentor to you, as Moses was to Joshua? It may be a pastor, a Bible study teacher, a parent, a friend, or even an author who has made an impact on your life. How does this person point you to Jesus, and how can you transition from looking to your mentor to looking to Jesus and staying in the tent even after your mentor leaves?

_____

_____

_____

_____

_____

_____

_____

_____

_____

_____

_____

_____

Action: Intentionally schedule "tent time" to be in God's presence every day over the coming week. Pray about what God would have you study and learn, the areas where He wants to see you grow, and what prayers He wants you to trust Him to answer.

Chapter Two Notes

CHAPTER THREE

Movement Mindset #3— Be Positively Different

But Caleb quieted the people before Moses and said, "Let us go up at once and occupy it, for we are well able to overcome it."

—Numbers 13:30

Out of the 600,000 slaves God delivered from Egypt, only Joshua and Caleb made it all the way to the promised land. They followed God and were able to claim their divine destination. We look to these guys in reverence and awe. They are an example of how moving with God can reshape our lives for the better, but they also show how life with Christ means getting used to being different.

Moving with God means that you're going to be different from those you are familiar with, those you do life with, and those who know you the best—as was the case with Joshua. It also means daring to bring a different perspective, a different outlook on life. It means daring to trust God when no one else does. People moving with God are called to be different.

In Numbers 14, the nation of Israel stopped in their tracks. They stopped believing God, and their momentum came to a halt. They even threw up their hands in exasperation and depression, feeling like God had given up on them, all because God was asking them to be different.

Just prior to this, in Numbers 13, the Israelites had reached the borders of the promised land. God instructed them to send twelve spies into the land to scope it out. Now, it's important to remember all that God had brought the Israelites through. In His name, they had conquered kings and seen miracles. They had been given the Ten Commandments and instructions for the temple, everything they would need to inherit their new home. They were on the precipice of receiving their promise. They were on the verge of victory, so when God said to send twelve spies, they did it.

But the spies came back with bad news. The people living in the promised land were too big, too fierce. Israel would never win. The promised land would never be theirs.

Two of the spies, Joshua and Caleb, had a different perspective. They believed that God would see them through to victory. They pleaded with the people, begging them to see that God was with them, but it was no use. The people of Israel gave up—*God is letting us down*—and an entire generation of Israelites lived and died in the wilderness, right on the edge of God's very best for them.

The Human Condition

The human mind delights in finding problems. Look at our world. Look at our country. There are plenty of reasons to be negative, to be doubtful of our future, and to believe that God is going to let us down. We look around and think, "The world is out of control!" We brace ourselves for bad things to happen.

Moving with God means ditching that negative attitude. It means believing for better things and trusting the One who is in control. Jonathan Sacks wrote about the characteristic of positivity in nations:[13]

Harvard University professor David Landes wrote a book called *The Wealth and Poverty of Nations*. The 500-page volume was a study of how some nations are extremely wealthy and prosperous, while others are impoverished. He came to one conclusion. "Why are some nations prosperous? Why are some other nations not prosperous? Because they are optimistic. Not because they are always right. But because they are always positive. Even when they are wrong. They are positive."

I think that we all want to be positive, but there's a breakdown somewhere between what we *want* and what we actually *do*.

Comedian Jack Handy wrote a book called *Fuzzy Memories*. One of the anecdotes went like this:[14]

There used to be this bully who would demand my lunch money every day. Since I was smaller, I would give it to him. Then I decided to fight back. I started taking karate lessons. But then the karate lesson guy said I had to start paying him five dollars a lesson. So I just went back to paying the bully.

It's a funny illustration, but sometimes that is how we are! We want to get out of our negativity until we realize how hard it is. The human condition is prone to negative things. A news link that is negative is more likely to get our clicks than one that is positive. A study conducted by researchers Marc Trussler and Stuart Soroka found evidence to support this:[15]

> Trussler and Soroka invited participants from their university to come to the lab for "a study of eye tracking". The volunteers were first asked to select some stories about politics to read from a news website so that a camera could make some baseline eye-tracking measures. It was important, they were told, that they actually read the articles, so the right measurements could be prepared, but it didn't matter what they read. ... The results of the experiment, as well as the stories that were read most, were somewhat depressing. ... The researchers present their experiment as solid evidence of a so called "**negativity bias**", psychologists' term for our collective hunger to hear, and remember bad news.

Negative news travels through culture and communities at lightning speed. How do we live as positive-news people in a bad-news world? How do we dare to be different?

From Praise to Pessimism

In the book of Deuteronomy is what many scholars believe to be a collection of five sermons that Moses preached before he died.[16] Moses recounted the forty years of struggle in the wilderness, and we believe that Numbers 13 is Moses' commentary on Deuteronomy 1. It's as if he were saying, "Here is what really happened."

> *The LORD spoke to Moses, saying, "Send men to spy out the land of Canaan, which I am giving to the people of Israel. From each tribe of their fathers you shall send a man, every one a chief among them." So Moses sent them from the wilderness of Paran, according to the command of the LORD, all of them men who were heads of the people of Israel.*
> *—Numbers 13:1–3*

When we're in the midst of major life change—maybe we're enrolling in school, starting a new job, dating a new person, or whatever it may be—we tend to examine where we're going. We look at all of the details and weigh all of the information, and sometimes we find that the more we check things out, the more we get freaked out! Sometimes we are so busy investigating that we investigate ourselves right out of an amazing opportunity. When this happens, we undermine the life of faith God wants for us.

The spies eventually returned to Moses and Aaron and all the people of Israel, and they recounted what they saw (Numbers 13:25–33). They shared that the land was fertile, flowing with milk and honey, and the fruit was so big that it required two people to carry it.

But as they continued to analyze and dissect God's promise, the news (as it still does today) trended toward the negative. The people dwelling in the land were strong. The cities were fortified and very large. Many of Israel's enemies lived in or near the promised land.

> *But Caleb quieted the people before Moses and said, "Let us go up at once and occupy it, for we are well able to overcome it." Then the men who had gone up with him said, "We are not able to go up against the people, for they are stronger than we are."*
> **—Numbers 13:30–31**

They saw the signs, and they still didn't believe. What's amazing is how quickly their spirit changed. They went from singing a song of praise in Exodus 15 after God worked the miracle at the Red Sea to a position of fear, dread, and hopelessness. It was like they had all the faith they could ever need on Sunday, but they forgot it by Tuesday.

> *So they brought to the people of Israel a bad report of the land that they had spied out, saying, "The land, through which we have gone to spy it out, is a land that devours its inhabitants, and all the people that we saw in it are of great height."*
> **—Numbers 13:32**

This is where we start to see Israel's logic really cave to fear. The spies claimed that the land was devouring its inhabitants, but didn't they previously state that the people living there were flourishing and strong? I call this an irrational calculation. It just doesn't make sense. Either the land devours the inhabitants, or the land is prosperous. It can't be both.

We do the exact same thing. We make these irrational calculations. The reality is that the majority of things we worry about never even happen, yet we allow worry to consume our thoughts and guide our steps. It's why insurance companies are booming and why our lives are so monotonous. We don't live by faith; we live by fear.

> *And there we saw the Nephilim (the sons of Anak, who come from the Nephilim), and we seemed to ourselves like grasshoppers, and so we seemed to them.*
> *—Numbers 13:33*

I call this an unsubstantiated assumption. They assumed that to these big, powerful sons of Nephilim, the people of Israel were nothing more than grasshoppers to be stomped out. But I guarantee that they didn't *ask* the sons of Nephilim if this perspective was accurate! They just assumed.

> *Then all the congregation raised a loud cry, and the people wept that night. And all the people of Israel grumbled against Moses and Aaron. The whole congregation said to them, "Would that we had died in the land of Egypt! Or would that we had died in this wilderness! Why is the LORD bringing us into this land, to fall by the sword? Our wives and our little ones will become a prey. Would it not be better for us to go back to Egypt?" And they said to one another, "Let us choose a leader and go back to Egypt."*

Then Moses and Aaron fell on their faces before all the assembly of the congregation of the people of Israel. And Joshua the son of Nun and Caleb the son of Jephunneh, who were among those who had spied out the land, tore their clothes and said to all the congregation of the people of Israel, "The land, which we passed through to spy it out, is an exceedingly good land."

—Numbers 14:1–7

In this passage, Joshua offered a reality check: "The promised land that we have been waiting for is an exceedingly good land." It was better than they could have dreamed. It showed God's love, providence, and blessing, and the people of Israel were about to throw it away because of their fear and doubt.

This is why negativity is so detrimental. God wants to do good in your life. Getting to that place of good may be hard, and it may cost you something. But in the end, after all the fighting and praying and fasting and seeking Scripture, His promise for you is *exceedingly good.*

Joshua went on:

If the LORD delights in us, he will bring us into this land and give it to us, a land that flows with milk and honey. Only do not rebel against the LORD. And do not fear the people of the land, for they are bread for us.

—Numbers 14:8–9

Please note that Joshua first tied rebellion to fear in this passage. Yes, sexual immorality, stealing, murder, and lying are acts of rebellion, but they are all simply fruits of a deeper rebellion: the spirit of fear. We fear that God does not want what's best for us, so we refuse to believe in Him. We then take matters into our own hands, seeking the good things from life with our own wicked imaginations.

Your problem is not sexual immorality; it's that you fear that God will never provide you with the intimacy you need. Your problem is not stealing; it's your fear that God will not provide what you need or give you many things you want. One of the passages I regularly share with my church is found in 1 Timothy 6. There Paul told Timothy that God loves to bless us and provide us with an enjoyable life:

> As for the rich in this present age, charge them not to be haughty, nor to set their hopes on the uncertainty of riches, but on God, who richly **provides** us with **everything** to en-**joy**.
> —*1 Timothy 6:17* (emphasis added)

God wants you to enjoy what He provides, and He is not stingy. All other sins are the results of disbelieving God's good intentions for us. The real sin of the spies in Numbers 13 was a rebellion of terrible proportions. They refused to believe that God was good and generous and instead blamed Him for bringing them to a place where they assumed that they would die.

I wonder who reading this may be doing the same. Maybe you fear the future and believe that the challenges ahead of you are God's way of punishing you for your past. Identify that you may be giving yourself over to a negative mindset based on unsubstantiated assumptions and irrational calculations, just as the spies did.

Their protection is removed from them, and the LORD is with us; do not fear them.
—Numbers 14:9

Joshua had a high view of God's sovereignty. He believed and *knew* that God is God over all nations, all people, every corner of the world. He knew that God would move and work to bring the people of Israel to what He had promised them.

How did the people respond? They wanted to kill Joshua:

Then all the congregation said to stone them with stones. But the glory of the LORD appeared at the tent of meeting to all the people of Israel.
—Numbers 14:10

The text goes on to say that this made God mad. He told Moses that He was going to kill them all and start a new nation through Moses. Moses' response was to remind God of His own words:

The LORD is slow to anger and abounding in steadfast love, forgiving iniquity and transgression, but he will by no means clear the guilty, visiting the iniquity of the fathers on the children, to the third and the fourth generation.
—Numbers 14:18

In this passage, Moses basically told God, "You are a gracious and compassionate God, showing mercy to thousands of generations. Don't forget that!" And God listened.

Some theologians have a problem with passages like this. Did God forget what He had said? Of course not. Scripture regularly speaks to us in human terms about God's unfathomable nature. Otherwise, we would struggle to relate to Him. Instead of trying to identify systematic theological facts about God, we should look at this passage for what it reveals concerning our relationship to God.

There are facts you know that are not presently in your mind. Moses was simply putting back into the mind of God what He had already said. Moses did this because he was familiar enough with God's words to recall and repeat them. We can do this as well! Take hold of God's promises concerning your life and bring them to His mind. You will be amazed at how things start changing.

> Then the LORD said, "I have pardoned, according to your word. But truly, as I live, and as all the earth shall be filled with the glory of the LORD, none of the men who have seen my glory and my signs that I did in Egypt and in the wilderness, and yet have put me to the test these ten times and have not obeyed my voice, shall see the land that I swore to give to their fathers. And none of those who despised me shall see it."
> —*Numbers 14:20–23*

Instead of wiping out the nation of Israel, God chose to forgive their sin. But He also determined that none of the men who had seen His glory and all of the signs and wonders He had done up to that point would see the land He had promised them. Instead, He would give the land to their children and their children's children.

He made two exceptions: Joshua and Caleb. The spies who dared to trust that God would make them victorious were the only two of the original 600,000 who would enter the promised land.

Good Advice Versus Good News

Here is my problem with this passage: we may assume that this passage is simply filled with good advice. It's advice that I've actually offered to you in this chapter. Be positive. Turn that frown upside down. Believe when you can't believe, and then believe even more. This passage is just chock-full of great advice, and every sermon I've heard on Numbers 13 and 14 has ended with this commission to the people of God: "Be like Joshua. Be like Caleb." This kind of message works because it is, again, good advice. I could give these pieces of advice to you in a list.

1. In matters of faith, resistance can arise from the important people in your life, the chiefs and the heads of families. These passages show that the power players and wisest of them went into the land and came back with a negative report. It shows that sometimes the people who are supposed to be the most knowledgeable or the most trustworthy get it wrong. Sometimes the most important people in your life will resist or complicate the path God has given you. Knowing this is good advice!

2. In matters of faith, the majority is probably wrong.

If you look at every instance of voting in the Bible, you'll find a bunch of disappointment. Every vote went bad. We see this today in our nation. People rely on those with money and on the power of government more than on God and the power of the Holy Spirit. We see it in churches, too. Congregations will vote themselves right out of an opportunity! They let fear get in the way of change and what God may do. This passage shows us how the majority usually gets it wrong, and that, too, is great advice.

3. Negative news is part of the human condition. Resist it! A pastor I know who majored in journalism in college once told me, "The first thing they teach you in college as a journalism major is that good news doesn't sell. Nobody wants to hear about 3,253 flights that landed safely last night. They want to hear about the one that had a problem, the one in which people almost died—or *did* die. Nobody wants to hear that 360 million Americans had a pretty average, ordinary day yesterday. We want to hear about that one dude that did the unthinkable thing that tells us that this world is going to pot tomorrow."

The passage in Numbers echoes this. The people of Israel didn't care about the good news. They fixated on the bad news. Negative news is part of the human condition, and this is good to know. It's good advice!

4. Negativity leads to irrational arguments and unsubstantiated assumptions. You start to think crazy thoughts and begin to exclude yourself from the possibility of what God could do in your life. This is what negativity does. It happens to all of us, and awareness of this fact is good!

5. Negative people get what they believe. If you send a negative person to research and report back on an opportunity, you're going to get a negative report. The consequence of this in the Numbers passage was that an entire people died in the wilderness. Think about that. Negativity brought about the exact end that the people were so afraid of. Knowing this is good advice!

What If There's More to Hear?

The common advice here is to be like Joshua. Just be a positive, God-focused follower and dare to trust in the midst of so many what-ifs. That's what we tell people, but here's the problem: it's hard to be like Joshua. We'd be exactly like him for 36.5 hours, and then we would fail again. Then we would turn negative again, and all of the pieces of advice we were given would rear their ugly heads and become an issue again.

Yes, being like Joshua is a good thing. It's good advice. But I can't preach that. I'm not here to give you good advice. I'm here to proclaim good news.

The good news is that two thousand years ago, the true Joshua showed up and did what none of us could do. He believed God perfectly. He obeyed God absolutely. He trusted God all the time. He did for you and me what we were incapable of doing ourselves. His name is Jesus, and He is the one who conquered our true enemies so that we can rest in His finished work.

Something significant happened to Joshua in Numbers 13 if we take time to look closely. The Bible tells us the names of the men sent to spy out the land. The list includes Hoshea, son of Nun (Numbers 13:8). Later in the passage, we learn that "Moses called Hoshea the son of Nun

Joshua" (Numbers 13:16).

Hoshea means "salvation."[17] Joshua means "YAHWEH is salvation" or "Jehovah-saved."[18] Moses put Jehovah before all else, making it clear that this man Joshua had help from above. It's as if Moses were saying, "I don't want you thinking that you are going to do this on your own, Joshua. The Lord is going to do this."

That's what happened for Joshua. The best solution to unsubstantiated assumptions and irrational calculations in your life right now is divine intervention. The Lord is going to do for you what you can't do for yourself. The Lord is going to make it possible for you to get what Joshua earned. The reason the Lord will do this is because He knows (better than you do) that you cannot save yourself.

The gospel isn't about doing better, trying harder, and praying more. The gospel is that *Jesus did it completely*. Jesus finished the work of our salvation and the spiritual victory over sin, hell, and death on the cross. He took our sin upon Himself so that we could take up His righteousness by faith and advance in confidence through life, despite any threat the enemy seems to present.

Good News for Doubters

When Jesus rose from the dead, one of the twelve wasn't there. The poor guy has been called "Doubting Thomas" for 2,000 years because he missed one church meeting. When Jesus appeared to Thomas, the Lord said, "Put your finger here; see my hands. Reach out your hand and put it into my side. Stop doubting and believe" (John 20:27 NIV).

We like to give Thomas alone the reputation of the one who doubted God, but that wasn't the case:

> Now the eleven disciples went to Galilee, to the mountain to which Jesus had directed them. And when they saw him they worshiped him, but some doubted. And Jesus came and said to them, "All authority in heaven and on earth has been given to me. Go therefore and make disciples of all nations, baptizing them in the name of the Father and of the Son and of the Holy Spirit, teaching them to observe all that I have commanded you. And behold, I am with you always, to the end of the age."
> —*Matthew 28:16–20*

These are people who saw Jesus alive after He was dead, and they still doubted. This is why we share the gospel. It's *good news*. You don't get what you deserve. You get what Jesus earned. We doubt, and He still makes a way. We're negative, and He still comes through.

> Furthermore, because we are united with Christ, we have received an inheritance from God, for he chose us in advance, and he makes everything work out according to his plan.
> —*Ephesians 1:11 (NLT)*

Moses blew it on several occasions, and God still used him. David killed a man and stole the man's wife, yet he was considered a man after God's heart. God took one of the babies David so wrongly fathered and turned him (Solomon) into the greatest king ever on the face of the earth.

God doesn't just use your good stuff, but also your bad

stuff, for the glorious purpose for which He created you before the foundations of the world. That's what the Bible teaches us. That is good news.

> And because of his glory and excellence, he has given us great and precious promises.
>
> —*2 Peter 1:4 (NLT)*

It's because of His glory and His excellence. It's not your glory. It's not your ability to take to heart good advice. It's not your perfectionism. It's because of Jesus' glory and His excellence. These are the promises that enable us to share in His divine nature and escape the world's corruption caused by human desires.

Joshua was not the only picture of our salvation in this passage. Caleb was standing strong in the promises of God with him. Actually, he spoke up first! If Joshua represents Jesus in this passage, who does Caleb represent? I believe that a small textual detail gives us a clue:

> And none of those who despised me shall see it. **But my servant Caleb, because he has a different spirit** and has followed me fully, I will bring into the land into which he went, and his descendants shall possess it.
>
> —**Numbers 14:23–24** *(emphasis mine)*

The text says that the grumbling and disbelieving generation would not enter the promises of God. These are the 599,998 orphans in the story who missed out on the billionaire's plans. The text goes on to stipulate that Caleb would be brought into the land because he had a "different spirit" from those disbelieving ten spies.

Caleb represents those who have the Holy Spirit dwelling in them by faith. His different spirit was one of faith and belief in spite of what the rest of the nation said. His different spirit enabled him to be positive in the face of negative circumstances. Do you have a different spirit from the people of your generation? The good news is that you can, by faith in Jesus Christ, have that different spirit.

More Than Sins Forgiven

The common Sunday-school answer to why Jesus died on the cross is "to take our sins away," but the theological reason goes much further. Jesus did not die simply to take away the bad things you've done and thought in your life. If that were the case, being human would simply be a matter of avoiding bad things at all times. But godly living is so much more than that! Jesus died to take away your sin *and* to cleanse you and make you a temple of the Holy Spirit. The Holy Spirit is not positivity or a life force or some sort of Jedi empowerment by which you manipulate the world around you. The Holy Spirit is a person, the third person of the Trinity.

Joshua and Caleb entered the promised land, and they had children. Those children were the beneficiaries of Joshua's and Caleb's faithfulness. To those who are born again by the Holy Spirit, to those who place their faith and trust in Jesus for the forgiveness of sins, to them—to *you*—are given the benefits of Jesus' faithfulness.

Jesus made it possible for the Holy Spirit to do in you what you are incapable of doing yourself. Don't be like

Joshua. Believe in Jesus, receive the Spirit, and allow Him to work through you.

Be Ready for the Inevitable

Let me be clear and stubbornly truthful here: no matter what you do, accomplish, acquire, or achieve, there will always be a voice of negativity ready to speak into your heart. I have seen our church grow consistently for seventeen years. Every year, I have watched new people take leadership roles and find their gifts. I have watched people show up dead drunk on Sunday mornings, only to meet Christ, become disciples, take on more responsibilities, and eventually plant a church (yes, a true story!).

Even with all of the positive things that have happened, we have encountered negativity from the very places I mentioned earlier in this chapter. I've grown to be completely unsurprised by it, yet it can still bother me. This is why going slowly through the Scriptures and spending tent time in God's Word has been so crucial.

God's best warriors, from Joshua to Elijah to Ruth and Elizabeth to Peter and Paul, all had moments when negativity was the news of the day. We see their stories in hindsight with 20/20 vision, but they experienced them in real time. Their stories are on the pages of Holy Scripture in full color so we can see their faults, failings, temptations, and troubles and press on as they did.

You won't be loved by everyone, no matter what you do, give, or say. In Luke 6:26, Jesus said, "Woe to you, when all people speak well of you, for so their fathers did to the false prophets." That verse reminds me that a voice of negativity is not necessarily a voice of truth. Press on and see your champion Jesus at the finish line, coaching you onward. You will finish. You will win.

Chapter Three Questions

Question: Do you tend to focus more on bad news or good news? Do you view the world through a lens of pessimism, negativity, and despair, or do you stay focused on God's unchanging character and the ways He is at work in the world through the ultimate good news of the gospel? What are some practical ways to combat the culture's continual obsession with negativity?

_____

_____

_____

_____

_____

_____

_____

_____

Question: Do you make decisions based on faith or fear? Describe a time when you talked yourself out of taking a step of faith because of worry or irrational calculations. What are some things that you tend to assume without seeking God's plan for you?

_____

_____

_____

_____

_____

_____

_____

_____

_____

_____

_____

Journal: *God doesn't just use your good stuff, but also your bad stuff, for the glorious purpose for which He created you before the foundations of the world.* Journal about a way in which you have seen God take a failure or difficulty in your life and use it for His own glorious purpose.

_____

_____

_____

_____

_____

_____

_____

_____

_____

_____

_____

_____

Action: What is an arena in which you need to be positively different? Is your school or workplace full of negativity? Is your church struggling with doubts and fears about the future? Do you have family members trapped in discouragement? Where can you take God at His word and be the Joshua or Caleb who boldly proclaims who God is and what He can do?

Chapter Three Notes

Movement Mindset #4— Be Seasonal

Let the LORD, the God of the spirits of all flesh, appoint a man over the congregation who shall go out before them and come in before them, who shall lead them out and bring them in, that the congregation of the LORD may not be as sheep that have no shepherd.

—Numbers 27:16-17

If you've ever tried to read the Bible all the way through, you know how hard certain sections and books can be. It's as if the action moves right along until you get to the middle of Exodus. It gets worse in Leviticus. Believe it or not, Numbers may win the prize for the most-skipped book in the Bible.

The reason why the book is called *Numbers* is because it includes two censuses. There was a counting of people who came out of Egypt and another counting of the people who were about to go into the promised land. Thrilling content, right?

This book really matters a great deal to the narrative of Scripture. Numbers takes us on a journey from one season of life to another. It chronicles the past and then looks to the future. But living through a seasonal change isn't always fun.

I just turned forty years old, and I was reading my journal from my thirties. It was embarrassing. I couldn't believe that I had struggled with what seemed like such insignificant problems. To make matters worse, I found my college journal and began to read what I put in there. Talk about shame! I literally could not believe what I thought were problems back then. Then a thought came to me. When I'm fifty years old, looking back at my journal from my forties, what will I think?

No matter what age we are, we will never be as wise or smart as our future selves. At the same time, the future—change—is scary. New seasons of life are uncomfortable. It's why so many churches get stuck with the same songs, the same pews, and the same people in the congregation for years.

The reason new seasons can be scary is that they force us to change in ways that will prepare us for where we are going rather than where we've been. They force us to ask, "Do I have what it takes for this new season? Did I make a mistake going in this direction?"

But the story in Numbers shows us that new seasons are reminders of new mercies. Every child of the living God who believes in Jesus is chosen and precious to the heavenly Father. You do not have to be afraid, worried, and stressed about this new season because God has you in the palm of His hand. He has new mercies lined up for you in your new season, and those mercies are new every day.

It's as if God were saying, "I just can't wait to give you more mercy." Did you make mistakes last night? There are new mercies. Did you ruin an entire year? New mercies. God doesn't bring you to new seasons to destroy you. He brings you to new seasons to employ you in what He has for you.

Seasonal Change

The book of Numbers starts off with a census. There were 603,550 men who could fight. All of these people came out of Egypt, and because of how things went down outside of the promised land, they lost their ticket in. Everyone over the age of twenty would die in the wilderness. That's forty years spent in the desert, right outside of God's promised land.

The hope that God offered them was that their children still had the opportunity to receive what they had lost. Their children could enter into the promised land and begin a new season for the history of Israel. See, even when we are faithless, God is faithful. The Israelites spent forty years living in the desert, trusting that God's mercies would renew.

Joshua was also struggling in this season of life. In Numbers 27, he was set to replace Moses, and he felt the pressure. Talk about a big role to fill! How on earth do you replace Moses? Joshua had to have been anxious about it. Up to that point, he had never led the people. He wasn't the one who got water from the rock or food from heaven. He had never parted a sea. Even so, he was the one God chose. He was being pushed into a new season. *Replace the man of God? How is that even possible?* We can relate.

In the 1990s, the NBA would draft eighteen-year-old kids right out of school. They would justify each one by saying, "He's going to be the next Michael Jordan. He's going to be a star." How many careers were crushed under that expectation? We were reminded with every failed phenom that there will never be another Michael Jordan.

I live in New England, and I remember when Tom Brady had to sit out a few games for a league-imposed suspension. The fans were panicked. *What are we going to do? How can we replace him?* But the truth is that there will never be another Tom Brady.

Billy Graham saw millions of people make the decision to follow Christ. As much as we want to replace him now that he's gone, there will never be another Billy Graham. You cannot simply replace one person with another. Even the Bible tells us this.

Deuteronomy 34:10 reads, "And there has not arisen a prophet since in Israel like Moses, whom the LORD knew face to face." Moses could not be copied. Joshua would have to enter into his own season of leadership.

The LORD said to Moses, "Go up into this mountain of Aba-rim and see the land that I have given to the people of Israel. When you have seen it, you also shall be gathered to your people, as your brother Aaron was, because you re-belled against my word in the wilderness of Zin when the congregation quarreled, failing to uphold me as holy at the waters before their eyes." (These are the waters of Meribah of Kadesh in the wilderness of Zin.) Moses spoke to the LORD, saying, "Let the LORD, the God of the spirits of all flesh, appoint a man over the congregation who shall go out before them and come in before them, who shall lead them out and bring them in, that the congregation of the LORD may not be as sheep that have no shepherd." So the LORD said to Moses, "Take Joshua the son of Nun, a man in whom is the Spirit, and lay your hand on him. Make him stand before Eleazar the priest and all the congregation, and you shall commission him in their sight. You shall invest him with some of your authority, that all the congregation of the people of Israel may obey. And he shall stand before Eleazar the priest, who shall inquire for him by the judgment of the Urim before the LORD. At his word they shall go out, and at his word they shall come in, both he and all the people of Israel with him, the whole congregation." And Moses did as the LORD commanded him. He took Joshua and made him stand before Eleazar the priest and the whole congregation, and he laid his hands on him and commissioned him as the LORD directed through Moses.

—Numbers 27:12–23

God Knows You Deeply

God knows you better than anybody else does. God knows you better than you know you. Because He knows you so well, there are going to be things that God does in your life that confuse you, things that perplex you. If you aren't careful, you will spend a decade crying to God, asking Him why, when all along He already knows what's best.

As soon as Moses found out that he wasn't going into the promised land, he prayed to "the LORD, the God of the spirits of all flesh" (Numbers 27:16). This is the only time that particular name for God appears in the Bible. Moses acknowledged that God is God over the desires and longings and fears of the flesh. He recognized that while he didn't have all of the information, God did. God knows the inner spirit of each and every person. He knows you. We all know that there are different "spirits" in people. Some people have the spirit to run a Fortune 500 company, but not the spirit to teach kindergarten. Some people have the spirit to stand on a stage and talk, but not the spirit to give one-on-one counsel. Some people have the spirit to build houses and coordinate projects, but not the spirit to be spontaneous and artsy.

God knows what spirit is in you, and He has a phenomenal track record of assigning the right spirit to the right place. You are the right person with the right spirit for something God has planned for you. You are the right person with the right spirit to go on a specific journey, impact certain people, and leave behind an important and unique legacy. Believe it!

Here are the hard facts that our "chase your dreams" culture will not tell you. We don't get to choose when we are born, where we are born, or to whom we are born. We don't get to choose our race, gender, or appearance. All of these things are God's choice. You are where you are because of divine appointment, so it's time to stop complaining about where you are. God knows you better than you know you. He is good at this stuff. He doesn't make mistakes.

For we are his workmanship, created in Christ Jesus for good works, which God prepared beforehand, that we should walk in them.
—Ephesians 2:10

I'm a theologian who has spent the better part of three decades searching out truths from Scripture about the reality of the human condition. I want to tell you something that's going to pinch. You may not accept it at first, but hang tight. Here goes. The idea of free will is a facade. You don't have free will. Adam and Eve ruined it. The Scriptures say that since that time, the human race has been in bondage to sin. That means we are slaves to our fallen nature.

Jesus answered them, "Truly, truly, I say to you, everyone who practices sin is a slave to sin."

—John 8:34

Do you not know that if you present yourselves to anyone as obedient slaves, you are slaves of the one whom you obey, either of sin, which leads to death, or of obedience, which leads to righteousness?

—Romans 6:16

In spite of our condition, God weaves His goodness into our lives, brings us to Him, and gives us new hearts that have new affections and are *free* to make good decisions. With Christ in our lives, all of our God-given differences and the unique spirits that live in us can become powerful tools He uses to bring change and blessing to the world.

Back to Joshua. He was chosen to take over the people with whom Moses had been struggling for forty years. On top of that, he was going to get only some of Moses' authority. While Moses talked to God face to face, Joshua would have to go through a priest to find the will of God. His situation was complicated and overwhelming. All the while, Joshua must have been thinking, "I want to be like Moses." But God told him, "I don't need Moses. I need you."

God Wants a Christlike You

God wants you to be you, but He wants you to be Christlike. This nonsense that God loves you just the way you are is not biblical. God doesn't love you just the way you are. In fact, I bet you don't even love yourself the way you are. This is why you keep trying to improve, to change yourself, and to adopt new habits every turn of the new year. God loves you *in spite of* who you are, and He wants to transform you into a new you, a different you.

This means taking who we are and striving to be more like Christ. It means embracing differences in the body of Christ while, at the same time, we all try to be more Christlike. The Bible tells us in 1 Corinthians 12:12, "For just as the body is one and has many members, and all the members of the body, though many, are one body, so it is with Christ."

We are all one body, but we have different parts to play in the body. This is exactly how God intended it. Some of us are singers. Some of us are ushers. Some of us are deacons. Some of us are pastors. Some of us are plumbers to the glory of God. Some of us are teachers to the glory of God. There is no such thing as secular work for the people of God. The work we do is sacred because we are doing it as temples of the Holy Spirit.

The more Christlike we are, the more we will enter into our strengths and unique callings within the body of Christ. We embrace seasons of change because they bring us closer to who we are meant to be.

God Made You to Live Selflessly

Just like this transition into leadership wasn't actually about Joshua, your new seasons are not actually about you. They are about the people around you. Moses didn't pray that Joshua would lead and bring authority because Joshua was so great, but because the people needed direction! This is an important reminder for when we're stressing over the current season.

Embrace this really good news. You don't have to stress. It's not about you. It has nothing to do with whether or not you feel up to it. It has nothing to do with what you're getting out of it. It has everything to do with what you're giving and the call to live selflessly.

When we have children, a switch goes off in our brain. Suddenly we go from filling our lives with whatever *we* want to filling our lives with things that will bring happiness and security to our children. *I've got to live for my son, my daughter. I need to make sure that we have money, food, and shelter. I need to offer direction and help and comfort. I will give everything I have for this child.*

Why don't we make that switch in other areas of our lives? When you get married, make the switch. *I'm no longer living for myself. I will give everything I have for my spouse.*

When you work a job, make the switch. *I'm no longer*

doing this job for myself. I'm doing this job for the people
around me. I'm going to do my best so that these people
are helped. I will give everything I have to this job.

And certainly when you go to church, make the switch.
It's a game changer. So many people attend church because they believe that they are in a season of life when
they need to be blessed. But Jesus didn't come to bless;
He came to serve. It's time for us to make the switch and
give everything for our churches instead of expecting our
churches to give everything for us.

First Peter 4:10 reads, "As each has received a gift, use
it to serve one another, as good stewards of God's varied
grace...." The people moving forward are the people who
step forward. They're the people using their gifts in a self-
less way for the glory of God.

Jesus Triumphed Completely

We don't need to fear this season or the next because
the enemy has already been defeated. When Jesus died,
Satan's powers died with Him. Your guilt died with Him.
Your fears died with Him. Your shame died with Him.
Your sin died with Him. When He rose, your new life rose
with Him.

When God looks on you, He doesn't see your guilt,
shame, or sin. You win because Jesus won for you. You
are accepted by the only opinion that counts: your heavenly Father's. Know that He will see you through this
season and every season to follow. He has plans. He can
use you. Embrace new seasons and enter into a new, better
way of living.

WORKBOOK

Chapter Four Questions

Question: What new season have you recently entered or may you soon be entering? What is exciting about these changes? What is uncomfortable or scary? Do you feel prepared, or do you worry that you might have gone in the wrong direction?

_____

_____

_____

_____

_____

_____

_____

_____

_____

Question: What are some ways you have grown more like Christ since trusting Him as your Savior? What are some ways you need to grow in Christlikeness? What are your strengths, spiritual gifts, and particular callings for ministry?

_____

_____

_____

_____

_____

_____

_____

_____

_____

_____

Journal: Read Psalm 139 and Matthew 10:30–31. Reflect on how deeply God knows you. What evidence can you see of how He knows you better than you know yourself? Do you trust God's decisions regarding you? How can you honor Him by embracing the season in which He has placed you?

_____

_____

_____

_____

_____

_____

_____

_____

_____

_____

_____

_____

Action: Think about your relationships within your family, workplace, school, church, and community. Has your focus been on yourself or on how God can use you to serve others selflessly? What is one practical way you can be less selfish and more of a servant in each of these areas? Act on that idea this week.

Chapter Four Notes

_____

_____

_____

_____

_____

_____

_____

_____

_____

_____

_____

_____

_____

_____

_____

_____

_____

_____

_____

_____

CHAPTER FIVE

Movement Mindset #5— Be Encouraged

Have I not commanded you? Be strong and courageous. Do not be frightened, and do not be dismayed, for the LORD your God is with you wherever you go.

—Joshua 1:9

Discouragement is easy to find. Just turn on the news, talk to a few friends, or scroll through your favorite social media site. At the time I'm writing these words, the tragic news of NBA superstar Kobe Bryant and his daughter's deaths in a helicopter crash was flooding the airwaves. Discouragement is common to our lives even when we seek to move with God. Things don't go the way we want, plans fall through, and people fail us. We end up seeing every morning as a brand-new chance to be disappointed.

While many people focus on disappointment, I see God encouraging His people. I can't tell you how many times I've been part of a church that decided to take a spiritual assessment survey. People filled in the blanks, checked the boxes, added up their scores, and checked those scores against the results sheet. Then bam! Everyone discovered his or her spiritual gift.

That's when I started to ask myself, "What is God's spiritual gift?" I believe that God is the great encourager. Don't get me wrong—He is the best at every gift. But He has a unique, proven ability to take nobodies and encourage them to become mighty people. All of the people who did great things for God started out as unimpressive nobodies. Then God moved in with His ways of encouragement, and Moses, a guy hiding from past failings, led the people out of slavery. A guy named Gideon, who was hiding from foreign occupiers, became the mighty warrior God always saw him to be. In the New Testament, an insecure teen named Mary became the mother of God. Peter, an overwhelmed sinner who felt like he didn't deserve God, became the Church's boldest evangelist.

The word *encourage* means to put courage into somebody. It means to hearten, or to give heart to, someone.[19] One of my favorite movies is *Rudy*.[20] In it, this little five-foot-nothing guy dreams of being on the Notre Dame football team. He defeats all the odds because he has the heart of a champion. He makes the team and ends up with a heart-stopping tackle in the final game of his career. It's a glorious story of someone who has heart. I have a picture of the real moment hanging in my office, signed by Rudy himself. It reminds me never to give up and to fight through even when everything else around me tries to rip the courage right out of me.

God Is the Great Encourager

How many times do we need someone to give us heart? That's what God wants to do for His people. He wants to put heart into us, and He does this through the Holy Spirit. When Jesus described the Holy Spirit in John 14, He described Him as "the Helper":

> *But the Helper, the Holy Spirit, whom the Father will send in my name, he will teach you all things and bring to your remembrance all that I have said to you.*
> —*John 14:26*

Instead of *helper*, some translations use the word *comforter* or *encourager*. Think about that. The Holy Spirit is the comforter, encourager, and helper whom the Father has sent.

> *Let not your hearts be troubled. Believe in God; believe also in me.*
> —*John 14:1*

This is God's plan for His people. As I talked about in Movement Mindset #3, Jesus bled and died on a cross 2,000 years ago not only so you could be forgiven for all of the bad things you've done, but also so you could be a temple in which God Himself dwells as the Holy Spirit.

God encourages you through the Holy Spirit. God Himself is living in you, not just giving you positive words of affirmation, but actually nurturing you and giving you heart every single day.

If you've noticed, people in our world are desperate for encouragement. People are desperate to be lifted up. The problem is that many Christians believe that their spiritual gift is the gift of giving advice. We want to tell people how to do things better. We want to point out why someone's life stinks. We act like we have all of the answers, but I think that we would go a lot further as the people of God if, instead of giving our opinions, we were to encourage people to move toward the gifts and the calling God has for them in the place He has given them. If we were to do that, we would be like the Holy Spirit, giving people heart and encouraging them toward their very best.

Encouragement is the breath of God, and we live in a culture in which people are choking. They're choking on all of the bad and wrong and evil things in the world. I go to work and see people choking. I go to church, and people there are choking, too. We need the Holy Spirit! And we desperately need brothers and sisters who point us in that direction, who encourage us and remind us that God is with us.

The God who called you is faithful (1 Thessalonians 5:24). He will complete you (Philippians 1:6). These are just some of His many promises, so let's be people filled with encouragement for one another. Let's be the kind of people who surround others with encouragement and support when life hits unexpectedly. When people get the wind knocked out of them, let's help them to get back up. Let's point them to God so that He can put the heart back into them.

This is what happened in Joshua 1. Joshua had the wind

knocked out of him. Moses was dead. The guy who led an entire nation out of Egypt and spoke directly with God was gone. Joshua had the wind knocked out of him, but God didn't waste any time allowing Joshua to choke.

God told Joshua to get back up. He then spent eight verses (Joshua 1:2–9) encouraging him, heartening him, and helping him to enter into the incredible next season. It was only then that Joshua was able to move into this opportunity.

God is encouraging us now, at this very moment. There are three ways He does this: through His Word, through His promises, and through His presence.

God Encourages Us with His Undeniable Word

If you need encouragement, get into the living, breathing Word of God. Satan has done a con job on the Bible. He has convinced this culture that it's an outdated book. He has convinced Americans that we no longer need it. He has worked to undermine its value in public education. He has convinced many people in our pews that they can't understand it, so they don't bother to try. He has convinced us to put it on a shelf. He has done everything in his power to keep this book closed because he knows the power in those pages. He knows how those words can transform God's people. He knows how the Bible *encourages*.

For centuries, the established church worked to keep the Scriptures out of the hands of the common man for fear that such knowledge would threaten their authority. Men like John Wycliffe and William Tyndale put their lives on the line to get the Scriptures in the hands of everyday people so that all might know the will of God and hear His voice speak life and confidence into their spirits.

The Bible is not a book of laws for the sake of laws. It's not a series of do's and don'ts. It's good news. It's the story of Jesus. It's the hope for the world.

Moses had a face-to-face relationship with God, and in that relationship, God told him to write everything down. The first five books of the Bible are the result of this command from God. Moses captured everything. After he died, those precious manuscripts were protected by the priest. The reason God had Moses do this was because Joshua—and all of the believers who came after—would rely on those scripts. Joshua didn't talk face to face with God. He didn't have to. He had God's words on paper.

The same is true with us. For some of us, it's our dream to have a face-to-face encounter with God. We think, "If only I could talk directly to Him, then all of my questions would be answered!" But God had a different plan. He knew that it would be better to write down everything He had to say to us. He put it in black and white so we would always be able to access it, no matter the season, no matter where we are or what we are doing.

If you think about it, all of the big moments of life are put into writing. They're not done with face-to-face, handshake agreements. They're done with contracts and written words.

When you pay all that money to go to college and you spend late nights studying, reading, and working through the courses, you write it all down. You take notes on everything important, everything that you think you will need to remember.

When you buy a house, you write it down. You sign a stack of papers taller than any you've ever signed before, and you put money toward the agreement. You don't simply take the seller's word for it that the house is yours. You make it official with a written document.

We write down everything that's important in life, and God feels the exact same way. He doesn't want us to forget His words, so He put them in writing.

For whatever was written in former days was written for our instruction, that through endurance and through the encouragement of the Scriptures we might have hope.
—Romans 15:4

Our problem isn't a lack of respect for the Word of God. We have plenty of that. Our problem is remembering what it says, and that's exactly what led to the first sin. Consider the serpent's strategy with Eve (Genesis 3:1–5). His first question undermined her familiarity with God's Word: "Did God really say…?" With a subtle shift in the phrasing of God's words, the woman was taken captive in a poisonous conversation that led to humanity's tragic fall. Think of that. The reality of sin in our world is rooted in carelessness with the voice of God. When we choose not only to receive the truths of Scripture, but also to remember them, we deepen our communion with God as if He were right there, face to face with us, just like He was with Moses. Now that's encouraging.

God Encourages Us with Unchanging Promises

God gave Joshua a promise: "Every place that the sole of your foot will tread upon I have given to you, just as I promised to Moses" (Joshua 1:3).

This had to have been incredibly encouraging to Joshua, but if you know your Bible, you know that there was nothing new about this promise. It was actually a hand-me-down promise that God had originally made to a man named Abraham six hundred years prior.

God told Abraham to lift his eyes and look around, and He promised that all of the land Abraham saw would belong to his offspring. Can you imagine? God's promises are abundant and always encouraging, but there's a problem. The problem is never the promise. The problem is our inability to *believe* the promise.

Right now, all God is asking is for us to believe Him. He is saying, "Trust Me. Believe Me," because what we believe matters. People don't go to hell because of what they do; they go to hell because of what they believe. No one goes to heaven because of a list of good achievements. People go to heaven because of their belief in God.

Truly, truly, I say to you, whoever hears my word and believes him who sent me has eternal life. He does not come into judgment, but has passed from death to life.
—John 5:24

Be encouraged! It's time to believe God's promises and move into what He has for you.

God Encourages Us with Unconditional Presence

Before Joshua fought a single battle, before he even stepped onto the battlefield, he had the presence of God. He experienced the presence when he was in that tent with Moses, he felt it when he was sent as a spy into the promised land, and he welcomed it when he stepped into Moses' shoes.

God promised Joshua, "I will not leave you or forsake you" (Joshua 1:5). That promise was not just for Joshua, but for all of us. It doesn't depend on how well you perform. God's presence is with us always, whether we realize it or not!

Corrie ten Boom was a Dutch Christian living under the Nazi regime.[21] She and her family felt that it was their Christian duty to hide Jews from the Nazis. Eventually they were arrested. The entire family was placed in a concentration camp, and Corrie and her sister ended up in one of the worst camps. Every other member of her family died, but Corrie lived. She traveled the world to speak about God's faithfulness. One of her most powerful stories was when her family had just been arrested.

She told her father, "I don't think I will have the strength to be a martyr for God." Her wise father responded, "Corrie, let me ask you a question. If I want to take you on a train ride, when should I give you the money for the ticket? A month before? A year?"

"No," Corrie said. "You'd give me the money right before I needed to buy the ticket."

"The same is with God," he said. "He is with us, and

he has what we need exactly when we will need it. His presence is unconditional."

Encouragement for Today

God wants us to live encouraged, uplifted lives every day. The foundational key to experiencing His encouragement is to maintain consistent, two-way communication with Him. How do we speak with God in a two-way conversation? We open our mouths to pray for His Word and His will to be accomplished in our lives, and then we open our Bibles, expecting Him to speak to us through the Holy Spirit.

I made a commitment to spend time each day in God's Word. I do this because I need to hear from Him for myself. Time and again, no matter which book of the Bible I may be reading or the time of day I set aside to hear from God, His Word speaks to my situation and encourages me in innumerable ways. Sometimes I feel defeated, and the Lord leads me to a passage in which one of God's "heroes" felt the pain of his own failure and God lifted him out of it. Sometimes I feel intimidated by challenges or opposition, and the Word of God shows me how often God's greatest men and women faced terrible odds and triumphed with Him, even when they did not feel strong.

When you listen to God's voice through His Word, you get that river of encouragement—God's best gift—flowing into your heart. He wants us to move confidently, knowing that He will be there every step of the way, encouraging us with His Word, His promises, and His presence. He lived on this earth. He knows what it's like, and He is, at this very moment, breathing encouragement into your life, whether you accept it or not. Open the Bible. Read His promises. Sit in His presence. Welcome His encouragement and see where it will take you!

WORKBOOK

Chapter Five Questions

Question: Describe a time when you received needed encouragement. How did God encourage you? What or whom did He use to get your attention and give you courage to keep going?

_____

_____

_____

_____

_____

_____

_____

_____

_____

_____

Question: When have others tried to fix you through advice rather than encouraging you through prayer and the promises of God? Are you more apt to share advice or encouragement? How can you make encouragement your default mode in your interactions with others?

_____

_____

_____

_____

_____

_____

_____

_____

_____

_____

_____

_____

Journal: How have you experienced an awareness of God's presence in your most difficult moments? Write down your story and share it with someone this week. How can you know that God is with you even when you don't feel His presence?

_____

_____

_____

Action: Write out some of the verses and promises that God has used to encourage you throughout your walk with Him. Which ones would be encouraging for a hurting or struggling friend right now? Which ones do you need to memorize so that they can help you when you face discouragement again?

Chapter Five Notes

_____

_____

_____

_____

_____

_____

_____

_____

_____

_____

_____

_____

_____

_____

_____

_____

_____

_____

_____

_____

CHAPTER SIX

Movement Mindset #6—
Be Crazy

At that time the LORD said to Joshua, "Make flint knives and circumcise the sons of Israel a second time." So Joshua made flint knives and circumcised the sons of Israel at Gibeath-haaraloth.

—Joshua 5:2–3

Faith in God can be a crazy experience. I'm not talking about being weird at church because you've wrongly understood the Christian experience or being strange for the sake of being strange. I'm talking about the crazy times when God asks you to do things that just aren't normal. Things that aren't typical. Things your neighbors aren't doing. Things your parents never did. Things that will turn heads and get the rumor mill going.

Faith in Christ is a call to move toward a crazy existence. When I say the word *crazy*, I don't mean it in the sense of "mad" or "insane." I mean it in the sense of "out of the ordinary" or "passionately preoccupied," as when people are "crazy in love."

To be a follower of Jesus is to have a life outside of the ordinary. This is because of the principles you have, the values you follow, and the things you do because of those principles and values. If you are a follower of Christ, there are things you do on a regular basis—monthly, weekly, daily—that nobody else around you does. You are passionately preoccupied with the work of God. You are passionately preoccupied with what God wants for you, and it may look crazy to some people.

It's crazy to forgive people who have hurt you deeply. It's crazy to choose sexual purity in an age when the culture, the news, and every show on television and on Netflix are telling you to be sexually liberated. It's crazy to base every decision you make on a God you don't see. Christianity is crazy, and you're crazy for being part of it. The sooner you accept that, the sooner you can move from where you are to where God wants you to be.

In Joshua 5 and 6, Joshua was asked to do something totally crazy. Israel was gearing up for their first big battle to take the promised land, and at the end of Joshua 5, the commander of the army of the Lord showed up. He told Joshua, "Here's the battle plan. I want you to march."

I'm sure Joshua was thinking, "Yeah, we can do that. We'll march right into battle, right?"

But the angel had a different plan. "March around the city once."

This wasn't your typical military procedure. Joshua was probably a bit confused.

The angel continued: "The next day, march around the city again. And the day after that, and the day after that, for seven days."

Joshua had to have been waiting for the plan of attack, but it never came. Instead of charging the city on the seventh day, God wanted them to be silent before they blew their trumpets, and then the walls would come down.

The plan must have sounded crazy. I can almost hear Joshua asking the angel to prove that he was from God. But sometimes God asks us to do crazy things.

Maybe right now God is asking you to do something out of the ordinary. Your friends, your parents, and even your spouse may not like it, but God loves it, and He is calling for it. Maybe God is asking you to start tithing ten percent of your income. Maybe God is asking you to go to that job where you aren't appreciated and bring donuts and show kindness to people who aren't kind to you. Maybe God is asking you to forgive the person who did that unthinkable thing to you when you were 12. God asks us to do crazy things all the time. The question is: How do you respond?

Going Crazy

When you are asked by God to do something out of the ordinary, how in the world do you muster the courage to say "yes"? The craziest thing about Joshua 6 isn't that God asked Joshua to win a war by marching around a city. The craziest thing is that Joshua followed the crazy plan *exactly* and the walls came tumbling down.

The secret to Joshua's boldness has to do with how God had been preparing his heart. Joshua didn't just stumble across this courage and faith. It had grown within him for such a time as this.

I find that a lot of Christians want God to do something outside of them. *I want You to heal my sister. I want You to fix this problem. I want You to give me that job. I want You to get me married. I want You to send me a child.* A lot of time, we are focused on the things outside of us that we want God to do for us, but God is saying, "I want to do something inside of you first." We worry about the outside, but God is looking on the inside.

Before God does things on the outside of you, He wants important matters settled inside of you. There are things God wants to remind you of and teach you. There are things He wants imprinted on your heart so that they can never be removed. It's only when the inside has been worked on that you're in a position to say "yes" to the crazy things He asks of you. You say "yes" because you know who you are in God. When your inside is ready, your outside can move forward naturally.

Here's how God prepared the hearts of Joshua and the people of Israel:

> As soon as all the kings of the Amorites who were beyond the Jordan to the west, and all the kings of the Canaanites who were by the sea, heard that the LORD had dried up the waters of the Jordan for the people of Israel until they had crossed over, their hearts melted and there was no longer any spirit in them because of the people of Israel.
> —*Joshua 5:1*

Think of this moment in the history of Israel. This former slave nation had been turned into a conquering force in the world. God had shaped and molded them for forty years. Now they were ready to take ground!

They had been through a lot. They had wandered for forty years. They had seen miracles and lost their faith a number of times, and in the process, they'd lost their heart. God knew that in order to win the promised land, Israel would first have to get back their passion and zeal and then give that over to Him. They had to give Him their hearts.

At this point, Israel was getting all kinds of affirmation that the nations of Canaan were theirs for the taking. The path seemed clear. The runway was lit, and all they had to do was land the plane. Most armies would charge in.

But no, before there was a battle, God wanted the entire nation to be circumcised. God was saying, "Listen, first I need you to do something that traces all the way back to your heritage." He wanted them to remember where they had come from. They had always been a circumcised nation, but forty years in the wilderness changed things. God began to work on their hearts by bringing them back to their covenant through circumcision. He was reminding them who they were.

I used to think that Abraham and the Israelites had to get circumcised to be accepted by God, but it's the opposite. Circumcision was the sign of God's approval. A sign points to something. It shows which way is north or south. It designates places, businesses, and streets. A sign doesn't *do* anything; it simply acknowledges what is already there. Throughout the Bible, circumcision was not a way of anyone being made right with God. It was a sign that the person was *already* right with God.

Paul wrote in Romans 4:

> *He received the sign of circumcision as a seal of the right-eousness that he had by faith while he was still uncircumcised. The purpose was to make him the father of all who believe without being circumcised, so that right-eousness would be counted to them as well, and to make him the father of the circumcised who are not merely cir-cumcised but who also walk in the footsteps of the faith that our father Abraham had before he was circumcised.*
>
> **—Romans 4:11–12**

We get to heaven because of our belief. In Genesis 12, God came to Abraham (then called Abram) and told him to leave his father and mother and everything he was fa-miliar with. God told him to go to the land that He would show him, and Abraham went. Three chapters later, he was walking the land, and God promised to give it to his children. This was his heritage. Abraham received this promise. The Bible says, "Abram believed the LORD, and he credited it to him as righteousness" (Genesis 15:6 NIV).

It's important to note here that Abraham was not yet circumcised, yet he found God's favor. In Genesis 17, God told Abraham to circumcise his sons as a sign by which Abraham would know that he had been approved by God. The blood that was shed was the sign of God's approval.

Four hundred years later, Moses was called by God to go back into Egypt and rescue His people. In Exodus 4, something weird happened, something crazy. Moses was struggling with his calling. He felt that he wasn't the right leader for God's people, and he asked God to send someone else. Just when Moses *finally* went back to Egypt to rescue God's people from slavery, the angel of the Lord met him, sword in hand. The angel of the Lord was going to kill Moses.

> *Then Zipporah [Moses' wife] took a flint and cut off her son's foreskin and touched Moses' feet with it and said, "Surely you are a bridegroom of blood to me!" So he let him alone. It was then that she said, "A bridegroom of blood," because of the circumcision.*
>
> *—Exodus 4:25–26*

It was as if God were saying, "Moses, I can't have you doing this crazy thing for Me publicly until I know that I have your heart privately." Before we see God doing things outside of us, He has to do something inside of us. He has to seal the deal on our hearts so that we have His approval. How? In the Old Testament, He did it through the blood of circumcision. Now He does it through the blood of His Son.

Seeking Approval

We're all looking for approval from someone, every one of us, even the people who consider themselves rebels and the individualists who claim not to follow anybody. Everyone has someone he or she wants to impress. In America right now, the very group of people who declared that they were for personal freedom and no judgment are the ones running around "canceling" you if you aren't in lockstep with their view of how life should be lived. If you want their approval, you will quickly acquiesce.

Whose approval are you living for? How much do you do just to be liked by someone else? You probably dress a certain way to be liked. You probably do your hair a certain way to be liked. In your teens, you probably did some stupid stuff that you regretted in your twenties. You do your job a certain way to be liked. You interact with friends a certain way. Why? Because all of us want approval. Our constant need for approval from someone other than God is what ties us up in knots and robs us of our God-given purpose. It keeps us from moving in the direction He has for us.

When you chase the approval of someone else, there's a good chance that you'll end up, forty years from now, in a place you hate. When you spend your life living for someone else, there's a chance that you'll never figure out what exactly you were made to do and be on this earth.

God is calling you back. He is trying to show you that He has you winning the battle of Jericho. He has you possessing the land. He already approves of you, and that's all that should matter.

What would it look like if you were to receive God's gracious approval deep down inside of your heart? How would it change your marriage, your parenting, and your business relationships if you didn't feel the need to seek out everyone else's approval and could move forward confidently with the only approval you really need: God's?

His Son's blood was shed to show you that you're in. You're approved. He loves you and is proud of you, but you can't move forward with God until this is a reality in your heart. Abraham faced this. Moses faced this. The whole nation of Israel faced this, too, right before they entered Jericho.

> When the circumcising of the whole nation was finished, they remained in their places in the camp until they were healed. And the LORD said to Joshua, "Today I have rolled away the reproach of Egypt from you." And so the name of that place is called Gilgal to this day.
> —*Joshua 5:8-9*

That word *reproach* means "to taunt."[22] Lots of people think that "the reproach of Egypt" refers to their slave mentality, but that's not true. This generation wasn't a group of former slaves. The Bible makes it clear that this was the generation born in the wilderness. They never knew Egypt.

What you have to see is that Egypt watched the powerful nation of Israel go nowhere for forty years. Think of the taunts: "God helped you out of Egypt, but look at where you are now—stuck in the desert! Hope it was worth it!"

Many of us live with taunts in the back of our heads— taunts from childhood, from a teacher, from a parent or a sibling or a spouse, from society. We are haunted by the taunts that say we will never measure up, never get where we want to be, never move past the obstacles. God is saying, "Let Me cut deeply in areas no one else sees so you can find that My Son's blood is enough." That's the power of the gospel.

God's approval matters because if He approves of you,

no one else needs to. No one else can give you what you already have from God. It's settled. His approval is the most perfect, most fulfilling, truest approval there is. The Apostle Paul put it like this: "Who shall bring any charge against God's elect? It is God who justifies" (Romans 8:33). The New Living Translation reads, "Who dares accuse us whom God has chosen for his own? No one—for God himself has given us right standing with himself" (Romans 8:33 NLT).

In the book of Romans, Paul built the case for this reality. He wrote about Jews and non-Jews, and in Romans 2, he clarified that a true Jew isn't just someone with the right lineage, but rather someone who is truly rooted in who he is in God, someone whose heart is right with God. True circumcision is not merely obeying the letter of the law. It's not just cutting yourself. It's not blood for the sake of blood. It's the change of heart produced by the Spirit.

> For no one is a Jew who is merely one outwardly, nor is circumcision outward and physical. But a Jew is one inwardly, and circumcision is a matter of the heart, by the Spirit, not by the letter. His praise is not from man but from God.
> **—Romans 2:28-29**

God comes in and circumcises your heart. He cuts away that desire for affection from others, that desire for approval from the world, the desire to be liked, the desire to fit in. As He makes you right with Himself, your heart begins to seek God, not other people.

There is a sign that symbolizes everything I'm talking

about for us New Testament people, and thank goodness it's not circumcision. The sign we've been given to show that we are approved by God is baptism.

In him also you were circumcised with a circumcision made without hands, by putting off the body of the flesh, by the circumcision of Christ, having been buried with him in baptism, in which you were also raised with him through faith in the powerful working of God, who raised him from the dead.
—Colossians 2:11–12

Getting dunked in a tank of water in front of hundreds of strangers is the best way to proclaim that you no longer care about what others think of you. It's the best way to show that you know who you are in the Lord, and that is your identity forever.

Approval Through Passover

Israel didn't go from circumcision to fighting. They paused to focus on God. Joshua 5:10–12 tells us that they celebrated the Passover on the plains of Jericho. With that great city looming in front of them, they ate.

And the manna ceased the day after they ate of the produce of the land. And there was no longer manna for the people of Israel, but they ate of the fruit of the land of Canaan that year.
—Joshua 5:12

God had been sustaining them all this time with manna from heaven. He sustained them as He worked on them. But His work was coming to an end, so the nourishment changed. They were on their own to scavenge and forage for food.

There are probably a lot of things you can think back on as things God did for you when you were first saved that you no longer experience. Maybe you had a warm, fuzzy feeling all the time. Maybe your prayers were answered really quickly, and your relationships were more clear-cut. You still feel the Spirit in you, but not in the same way anymore. It takes longer for you to see answers to your prayers, and relationships with others are messy. You wonder, "Where is God? Why does my life get harder the longer I'm a Christian?"

It's God's way of growing you up. It's His way of getting you to realize that He has set you apart and sanctified you for His purposes and His plan. He has done a work inside you, and now it's time for you to go out and get food on your own. You don't need Him in the same way you needed Him before. If you read that passage of Scripture, you'll see that there is fruit waiting for you. There is nourishment in front of you; you just have to step out and find it.

This was a big step for Israel, but it wasn't just a time of relaxation. God had high expectations. In Leviticus 23, God was clear how He wanted the firstfruits of the promised land to be handled:

And the LORD spoke to Moses, saying, "Speak to the people of Israel and say to them, When you come into the land that I give you and reap its harvest, you shall bring the sheaf of the firstfruits of your harvest to the priest, and he shall wave the sheaf before the LORD, so that you may be accepted. On the day after the Sabbath the priest shall wave it. And on the day when you wave the sheaf, you shall offer a male lamb a year old without blemish as a burnt offering to the LORD. And the grain offering with it shall be two tenths of an ephah of fine flour mixed with oil, a food offering to the LORD with a pleasing aroma, and the drink offering with it shall be of wine, a fourth of a hin. And you shall eat neither bread nor grain parched or fresh until this same day, until you have brought the offering of your God: it is a statute forever throughout your generations in all your dwellings.

—Leviticus 23:9-14

God's proven acceptance of His people was twofold. He proved His acceptance of them through circumcision, and He proved His acceptance again by receiving their sacrifices during Passover.

You Have His Approval

In God's family, no one eats alone. We are accepted, and the Holy Spirit comes in and cuts deep into our hearts. He draws us together. He moves us to celebration, to rejoicing, to reflection. He accepts us, and His proof of that acceptance is His incredible presence in our lives.

Think about that. The Holy Spirit alive inside you is evidence that you are accepted. Your participation at the communion table, much like participation in Passover, is evidence that you are accepted. This acceptance is the underlayment of our faith. We can act in ways the world may think odd or unnatural because we do not need the world's approval or acceptance. We have these things in the house of our Father.

Let us reignite our hearts with God's love and fellowship. When we live from a position of already being approved by Him, there is nothing we can't do.

Chapter Six Questions

Question: What are some crazy, out-of-the-ordinary things you have done or are doing in obedience to God? Would others look at your life and think that you are normal by the world's standards or that you are different because of Christ? Why?

_____

_____

_____

_____

_____

_____

_____

_____

_____

Question: Have you ever felt ready to take a big step of obedience or to follow God in a new endeavor, only to have Him show you that you were not spiritually prepared for that next step? In what ways did God need to change your heart?

_____

_____

_____

_____

_____

_____

_____

_____

_____

_____

_____

Journal: Look over your prayer list or review your most frequent prayer requests. Are you focused on God doing or fixing something outside of yourself, or are you seeking for God to change your heart and prepare you for His plans? Write out your prayers for what you want God to do inside of you so that you will be ready for whatever He does outside of you.

_____

_____

_____

_____

_____

_____

_____

_____

_____

_____

_____

_____

Action: Read, write down, and memorize Romans 8:33–39. How would your life change if you were truly to operate in the belief that you are already fully accepted and approved by your heavenly Father?

Chapter Six Notes

_____

_____

_____

_____

_____

_____

_____

_____

_____

_____

_____

_____

_____

_____

_____

_____

_____

_____

CHAPTER SEVEN

Movement Mindset #7—
Be Constantly Moving Further

So now give me this hill country of which the LORD spoke on that day, for you heard on that day how the Anakim were there, with great fortified cities. It may be that the LORD will be with me, and I shall drive them out just as the LORD said.

—Joshua 14:12

Joshua and Caleb were two guys who moved with God all the way from slavery in Egypt to the promised land (Joshua 14). Out of 600,000 people, they were the only two who believed God's promises. They were the only two who trusted God in the face of obstacles and were able to experience the fulfillment of His promise.

After studying their story in great depth, I know one thing: I don't want to settle for a life that is dull and ordinary. I choose to believe that God is moving us forward to better things at all times. In Christ, there is no retirement until we pass from this life to the next. No matter where

God has you today, there's more ahead. Moving with God is never based on a permanent destination on the earth. We keep moving forward until He moves us into glory.

In the final lesson of this book, I want to focus on someone other than Joshua. I want to look at Caleb. He may be secondary in the number of mentions, but his faith and perseverance are a model for anyone who may feel like God has no more conquest for them to experience.

Joshua gets the spotlight in the narrative of Scripture while Caleb feels like an add-on. Joshua is mentioned 222 times, and Caleb is mentioned 36 times. Caleb didn't get the press. He didn't get the highlight reel or a book in the Bible named after him. It was Joshua who took over for Moses, not Caleb. But when the twelve spies came back after scouting the promised land, it wasn't Joshua who spoke up first. It was Caleb. Caleb quieted the people. Caleb dared to make a bold statement of faith. Caleb declared that the Lord would be with the people of Israel.

The name *Joshua* means "the Lord saves."[23] The name *Caleb* means "dog."[24] In the ancient world, they didn't love dogs the way we do. Dogs were scavengers. They were dirty and ignored. A verse in 2 Samuel gives a sense of just how little they thought of dogs in ancient times: "What is your servant, that you should show regard for a dead dog such as I?" (2 Samuel 9:8). Dogs were the lowest of the low; they meant nothing. That was the meaning behind Caleb's name. It didn't invoke greatness. It didn't inspire armies.

But Caleb shows us that ordinary people can do great things for God. If you feel left out, if you feel that life has been unfair, if you feel overlooked, then let Caleb be your inspiration. He can teach you better than anyone else what it means to move forward in faith, no matter what.

Then the children of Judah came to Joshua in Gilgal. And Caleb the son of Jephunneh the Kenizzite said to him: "You know the word which the LORD said to Moses the man of God concerning you and me in Kadesh Barnea. I was forty years old when Moses the servant of the LORD sent me from Kadesh Barnea to spy out the land, and I brought back word to him as it was in my heart. Nevertheless my brethren who went up with me made the heart of the people melt, but I wholly followed the LORD my God. So Moses swore on that day, saying, 'Surely the land where your foot has trodden shall be your inheritance and your children's forever, because you have wholly followed the LORD my God.' And now, behold, the LORD has kept me alive, as He said, these forty-five years, ever since the LORD spoke this word to Moses while Israel wandered in the wilderness; and now, here I am this day, eighty-five years old. As yet I am as strong this day as on the day that Moses sent me; just as my strength was then, so now is my strength for war, both for going out and for coming in. Now therefore, give me this mountain of which the LORD spoke in that day; for you heard in that day how the Anakim were there, and that the cities were great and fortified. It may be that the LORD will be with me, and I shall be able to drive them out as the LORD said."

And Joshua blessed him, and gave Hebron to Caleb the son of Jephunneh as an inheritance. Hebron therefore became the inheritance of Caleb the son of Jephunneh the Kenizzite to this day, because he wholly followed the LORD God of Israel. And the name of Hebron formerly was Kirjath Arba (Arba was the greatest man among the Anakim).

Then the land had rest from war.
—Joshua 14:6–15 *(NKJV)*

Caleb was 85 when he spoke those words. He was looking back on a life well lived. He had followed God with all of his heart, trusting God's word over man's, trusting God over popular opinion.

There's more to this story than meets the eye. Scripture is clear that Caleb was well aware of the enemy on that mountain. Joshua 14:12 reads, "...for you heard in that day how the Anakim were there..." (NKJV). The Anakim played a significant role in God's redemptive history. A few cross references help to clarify the picture Caleb's faith and victory provide for us.

Deuteronomy 9:2 describes the Anakim as "a people great and tall, the sons of the Anakim, whom you know, and of whom you have heard it said, 'Who can stand before the sons of Anak?'" Deuteronomy 2:11 gives us another name for the Anakim, "Rephaim." Stay with me through these difficult Old Testament names. The name *Rephaim* comes from the Hebrew for "ghosts of the dead."[25]

In other words, Caleb took on an ancient, fabled giant-people who were so intimidating, their enemies considered them ghosts. If you go back a few chapters in Joshua, you will find that these people remained in other parts of the land. Joshua 11:22 reads, "There was none of the Anakim left in the land of the people of Israel. Only in Gaza, in Gath, and in Ashdod did some remain." Did you pick up a familiar town in that list? It's Gath, where another giant of death, Goliath, came from later in Scripture. Goliath was conquered by a descendent of Caleb named David.

This is why I love Scripture. Every story points to the

ultimate story. Caleb's mountain-top conquest pointed forward to the shepherd boy who became king. David's conquest of Goliath pointed forward to King David's descendent, the good Shepherd, King Jesus. Jesus struck down the ultimate ghost of death and hell at the cross, winning our victory and securing our place in the family of God. Second Timothy 1:10 reads, "He broke the power of death and illuminated the way to life and immortality through the Good News" (NLT).

For forty years, Caleb dared to move with God. He wandered that desert. He fought those wars. He was a slave and later a conqueror. He never dared to stand still. He moved when, how, and where the Lord led him, and the impact that faithfulness had on his life is evident.

Friend, there's more for you than you have previously experienced. The life of faith doesn't end until the champion of our faith comes again. Until then, we must keep moving forward into the unknown areas of life, taking on the challenges that lie ahead and "looking to Jesus, the founder and perfecter of our faith" (Hebrews 12:2). I want to live in the ancestry of faith that Caleb and David modeled for us. I want to follow my champion Jesus to the mountain-top conquests that would intimidate others. I might have come a long way, but I want to keep moving.

Movers Don't Finish

When we move, we tend to think primarily about the finish line. *I'm going to eat healthy food so that I can lose weight. I'm going to wake up early so that I can write this book. I'm going to turn off social media so that I can be present at home.* We give goals to every big life change we make as a way to measure our success.

The problem is that once we cross that finish line and hit that goal, we stop. We achieve what we set out to achieve, then we're done. We plateau.

Scripture is clear: finish lines are for dead people. How do I know? Because every time I read about people finishing in the Bible, they're dead. In 2 Timothy 4:6–8, Paul wrote that he had run the race and kept the faith and that he would soon die. Acts 13:36 tells us that "David, after he had served the purpose of God in his own generation, fell asleep...." On the Lord's timeline, you're only done when you're dead.

Moving with God means that we must eliminate our self-made finish lines. It's not about doing something for a season. It's about doing what God calls you to do until He takes you home, no matter how long that is. Life is not about the product of your effort; it's about enjoying the journey. It's about aiming for a daily walk with God, not a goal that needs to be accomplished. As long as you're alive, God has something for you to do. He wants you to move forward now. Your race isn't finished.

Caleb lived this. He held to this promise for forty-five years. While in the wilderness, he watched everyone around him die. People he knew and loved faced their finish lines without receiving God's best for their lives and entering the promised land. How long would you last in those conditions? How long would you hold out before throwing in the towel and giving up, saying that it wasn't worth it?

Caleb stayed the course. He kept running. He

understood that life is all about waiting on God while you enjoy the process. It's about facing challenges, the giants of the land. It's about pressing on, refusing to give up, because you know that those who are still in the fight are blessed and God is not done with them yet.

Will You Keep Moving with God?

I have had the privilege of pastoring one church for the past eighteen years. I know from first-hand experience that you do not need to jump from organization to organization to encounter movement. In fact, I have found that by staying in one position and serving the Lord, the movement has happened in ways I could not have predicted.

When I was preaching the sermon series on which this book was based, our church was taking on a $10 million building project to restore an old jewelry manufacturing plant in Massachusetts and turn it into our new home. It was a long and arduous task, filled with many unexpected obstacles. Even so, I did not want this project to be a finish line for our church. The worst thing would have been for us to settle into our new digs, feel like we had made it, and then rest on our laurels until Jesus returns.

Our mission as a Church is not to build buildings, but to reach people who are far from God. According to my research, millions of new people are being formed every day, so the mission is never finished. God always has much more for us to accomplish.

What do you do when you're halfway through a major renovation project with your church? You plan to plant two more churches within a year of opening. Okay, that's not exactly what they teach you in seminary, but that's what we did. I felt that the best way to keep our church on the move with God was to plan something the New England area desperately needed: new churches.

I teach a leadership class every year in our church, and I presented the plan to the class while construction was underway. Amazingly, within nine months of our opening Sunday, we were sending more than seventy people out of our building to plant two new campuses of our church. I was overwhelmed by the spirit of those team members who were ready to set up church in schools every Sunday to make it happen.

You may be assuming that I'm a great motivator and leader, but I cannot take the credit. A move of God at a specific church gathering made it all possible. Our church has a monthly Wednesday night service for those who consider themselves fully vested in the church. During one particular service, the Lord led me to preach on a passage I've always loved, Isaiah 6. In that chapter, the prophet had just finished proclaiming six woes upon the nation for their immoral and corrupt ways. Greed, idolatry, sexual sins, and violence were the standard of the day, and Isaiah boldly confronted the sins of his people with woe after woe after woe in Isaiah 5.

But when you turn the page to Isaiah 6, it's the passage that tells of when Isaiah saw the Lord in the temple with the seraphim, who shouted, "Holy, holy, holy…!" (Isaiah 6:3). Smoke filled the place along with the train of His robe. In this passage, Isaiah presented a seventh woe for only one person: himself.

And I said: "Woe is me! For I am lost; for I am a man of unclean lips, and I dwell in the midst of a people of unclean lips; for my eyes have seen the King, the LORD of hosts!"
—Isaiah 6:5

The picture of God's prophet being overwhelmed with the presence of God is one to behold. Isaiah was forcefully chastising the nation for their sin in one moment. In the next moment, he was crushed by the weight of his own sin when he saw the real presence of the Lord in the temple.

At this point, you may think that God would start showing the prophet all of his faults, proving him unworthy of the work, but that's not what happened. Instead, after one of the seraphim cleansed Isaiah's lips with a coal from the altar (Isaiah 6:6–7), God spoke to Isaiah. His words were full of movement:

*And I heard the voice of the LORD saying, "Whom **shall I send**, and who will go for us?" Then I said, "Here I am! **Send me**."*
—Isaiah 6:8 *(emphasis added)*

What a moment! I shared with my congregation this simple truth from Isaiah's experience with the overwhelming presence of God: the closer you get to the Lord, the more motivated you are to go to the nations with His Word. An experience with God will produce in your spirit a heartfelt desire to *go* in His name to the people who need to hear His Word! Something powerful happened in our church that night. God birthed a *movement spirit* in our hearts, and we are still seeing the fruit of it to this day.

When You Move, Your Heart Changes

About a year after we planted those churches, I was invited on a mission trip to Guatemala with our director of pastoral care. I am ashamed to tell you this, but I didn't want to go. I arrogantly thought, "I'm doing missions right here! I don't feel called to the foreign mission field at all! I'm a church pastor, not a missionary." I'm really good at telling God what He shouldn't ask me to do.

I ended up going, kicking and screaming in my spirit the whole way. We flew Spirit Airlines, which has a notorious reputation for terrible service. We arrived in Guatemala with twenty-five enthusiastic members of our church and one miserable, hesitant pastor (yours truly).

Then we took a tour of Hope of Life, Guatemala and the work Carlos and Cheryl Vargas had been doing for over thirty years. Within moments, I was overwhelmed by the mission and efforts of God's people in that part of Central America. We met pastors and church leaders in remote parts of the country. We did service projects, fed villages, and ministered to hundreds of Guatemalans.

The week was exhausting. I still consider the Tuesday of that week the hardest day of work in my entire life. We dug trenches in the hard-rock sand for chicken coups, which was physically intense, but the life change was invaluable. The experience propelled us forward as a church in ways I never imagined.

During the week, a connection was struck up between our church and Hope of Life. The founder, Carlos Vargas, asked me to consider planting a church on the campus for his workers. This would be an English-speaking church geared toward those who live on campus and visit regularly to help empower them in Christ and shepherd them in the Word as they do the work of ministry.

Without hesitation, I said "yes." Today our church is establishing a location in Guatemala by faith and through the generosity of our people. One of our best young couples are quitting their jobs, selling their things, and relocating to Guatemala to lead the work there. I never would have predicted this! Planting a church in Central America? Sending Americans to live there permanently? Talk about *movement*!

During this process, the Lord reminded me of a conversation we had years ago. In my Bible college days, we used to have an annual week-long missions emphasis, with services at night to pray for and hear from missionaries. I had it settled in my mind that pastoral ministry in the United States was my calling, but during one of those weeks, I asked the Lord, "If You were to want me to go to another country and serve You, where would it be?" He instantly put a name in my mind: *Guatemala*. God reminded me of this moment about six months into planning the church plant, and I've been back to that country three times in this past year to live it out.

Not only does your heart change when you move with God; your mind is blown by His purpose and plan working out for you and through you over time in creative ways. Keep moving with God. Embrace the opportunities and seasons of your life with expectancy. Face the obstacles in front of you with confidence, hear God speak to you daily, and partake in efforts that the world may think are outlandish. God is for you, not against you! He has great things in store for you, but they aren't going to happen if you stay right where you are.

The mind of God is in the movement of God. Philippians 2 says so. There Paul unpacked the mind of Christ that was to be in the church at Philippi in the first century. What is that mind of Christ? Paul wrote in Philippians 2:6–11 that Christ *moved* out of His place in heaven with the Father as God the Son and *moved* into the human race. He *moved* from the cradle all the way to the cross, and then, finally, He *moved* into glory. The mind of Jesus is a mind submitted to moving in accordance with the plan and purpose of God. We are to have this same mind in us (Philippians 2:5).

WORKBOOK

Chapter Seven Questions

Question: Do you feel that your life is dull and ordinary in light of all you know that God can accomplish through you? Do you think that you have stagnated or plateaued in your walk with God? What needs to change in order for you to believe that God is moving you forward to better things at all times?

_____

_____

_____

_____

_____

_____

_____

_____

_____

Question: Do you feel left out? Do you feel that life has been unfair or that God has overlooked you? What encouragement can you derive from Caleb's story and example? What does God's view of Caleb reveal to you about His heart for you? How does that affect your perspective on your current circumstances?

_____

_____

_____

_____

_____

_____

_____

_____

_____

_____

Journal: In your journal, make a list of all the dreams, goals, and/or personal qualities that you have viewed as a finish line or a measuring stick to determine when you have "arrived." Ask God to show you which goals are in line with His plans and purpose for you. Then write out a prayer of surrender, acknowledging that you are not finished with your race as long as you live, even if your wildest dreams are fulfilled. Commit anew to serving the Lord until you breathe your last breath.

_____

_____

_____

_____

_____

_____

_____

_____

_____

_____

_____

Action: *An experience with God will produce in your spirit a heartfelt desire to go in His name to the people who need to hear His Word.* Read Isaiah 6:1–8. Ask God to touch you with His heart for those around you and in the world. Is there a specific person or group that comes to mind? What is something practical and meaningful you can do for them as a picture of God's love?

Chapter Seven Notes

EPILOGUE

When You Are *Forced* to Move

I can do all things through him who strengthens me.
—Philippians 4:13

I finished this book four weeks before the worldwide coronavirus pandemic ensued. In fact, I was in Guatemala getting our campus ready with some staff when I first heard that the virus had begun to infect people in the United States. We didn't yet know that the country would be turned upside down with the rest of the world in ways no one would previously have thought possible. Sometimes conditions in the world force you to move.

The COVID-19 pandemic revealed that life's uncertainties are a matter of inevitability, not chance. Embracing change and moving with God can empower you to live through both planned and unplanned transitions.

COVID-19 changed society, but it also forced the Church to move in ways we never would have chosen if we'd been left tucked safely in our comfort zone. We were forced to move from in-person gatherings with multiple ministry venues to digital spaces and technological tools to teach people about the faith.

For ten weeks, I preached to an empty auditorium, something I had done only a handful of times before to prepare a message for multi-site presentation. Our children's team transitioned their curriculum to online-only material. Our small groups instantly embraced Zoom and Google Hangouts calls. Instead of sharing communion in person, we shelved the practice in anticipation of coming together again at some point in the future. Our churches, our families, our nation, and our lives were forced to move, and it underscored the necessity of embracing a movement mindset even if you never *plan* on moving.

While the effectiveness of the lockdown will most likely be debated for a long time, there's no debate about our need to embrace movement. For our church, the transition to completely online ministry was seamless because we had been moving more ministry online for the last seven years. We already offered online church gatherings.

We continued our midweek Bible study because I had been doing that completely online since its inception three years earlier. It's a YouTube show called *The Deep End* that talks about current events and moves through Scripture, one book of the Bible at a time. In some ways, it has become my favorite moment of the week. That show was online and ready to continue right through the lockdown because we had embraced a movement mindset years earlier.

In the New Testament, Paul took the gospel to where people moved in and out. Ancient metropolitan and trade centers like Ephesus and Corinth were his strategic landing spots to preach the gospel. Today the trade route is digital, so our content must be strategically placed in that space. The point I'm making is simple: if you embrace a movement mindset now, you will be ready for the moments when life moves you without your permission.

For many of my pastor friends, there was a hurried scramble to get something online to offer their members in the first weeks of the crisis. I offered my help, and our tech teams taught them as much as they could, but for some it was too little, too late. I watched as those who formerly shirked moving forward with digital technology finally did just that because they had *no choice*. I do not say this to criticize them but to admonish you. Movement is part of the human experience, and ignoring it or avoiding it will never help you in the future.

Perhaps the greatest lesson of the coronavirus lockdown for me was a reminder that we are rarely ever ready to change, to venture into uncharted waters, to try something new. No, we have to *force* ourselves to do these things. What new venture have you forced yourself to embark on lately?

During a few weeks of the lockdown, I forced myself to embrace a different teaching technique, which I know will become a regular part of ministry going forward. I took a few cameras into the woods and filmed myself preaching on location. I did this with no film crew, inspired by one of my favorite shows ever, *Survivorman*. I preached in the woods about Israel's journey through the wilderness in order to relate it to the worldwide experience we were having. I was amazed at the reception of these videos. The "outdoorsy" people loved them, and I was able to connect with them on a whole new level. Moving makes room for more influence in your life.

I remember my own resistance to this venture. I felt weird about going into the woods without a camera crew and challenging myself to pull off a Les Stroud-style video while preaching. *No one does this, or at least I haven't seen it. Who am I to think that I can do this?* Those kinds of thoughts filled my mind. I was unsure. I was insecure. I was nervous. But I forced myself to do it anyway. Now I'm ready to do it again and again. It was awesome.

At the time of this writing, we are turning the corner on COVID-19, and our church has reopened, but I see many pastors and Christians dragging their feet to move on from this crisis. Do you see how hard it is to keep moving? The people who struggled to move *into* lockdown are now struggling to move *out* of it.

Stalling seems to be part of the human condition, and perhaps it is one of the unseen effects of the curse of sin. This is why you must ask God for the Holy Spirit, like the believers who prayed for boldness in preaching the Word and for miracles to be done in Jesus' name and were filled with the Spirit (Acts 4:29–31). The power of the Holy Spirit propelled Jesus to embrace the road to Calvary. Then the Holy Spirit propelled the gospel to stretch around the world through ordinary, unschooled men like Peter and John, servants like Philip, landowners like Barnabas, and strict Pharisees like Paul. They never stopped moving on from where and who they were, and because of them, much of the world has heard the gospel. The point is that you have to challenge—no, *force*— yourself to move. If you don't, you'll be ten years older and living the exact same life you were living before, and that's only if you're lucky. Worse, the world could change in an instant, and you would be ill-prepared to handle it. God does not want that for you. He wants you to "be ready in season and out of season" (2 Timothy 4:2). He wants to show you to a fearful world as evidence that there's no reason to fear when you live in His perfect love (1 John 4:18). Christians should be people who embrace every season because we know who made them and who oversees them.

While the earth remains, seedtime and harvest, cold and heat, summer and winter, day and night, shall not cease.
—Genesis 8:22

I'm asking myself right now, "What needs to change in me or through me?" I suggest that you do the same. Change and transformation are not simply spiritual values leading to character formation. They are mindsets that empower the formation of your entire life.

I pray that some of what I have presented to you in this book helps you to look forward in faith so that spiritual muscle is developed and strengthened to take on whatever challenge is headed your way. Remember the words of the Apostle Paul to the Philippians from a Roman prison: "I can do all things through him who strengthens me"

(Philippians 4:13). That passage comes alive when you consider that this was the second time Paul was on lockdown for the sake of the gospel. The first time was in that very city of Philippi, where God miraculously delivered Paul and Silas through an earthquake.

When Paul wrote Philippians, he was addressing the church that witnessed the earthquake deliverance, but this time, no earthquake deliverance was in the works. The fact that Paul could not physically move from city to city did not stop him from embracing the (at the time) technological advancement of writing. You could say that we have the book of Philippians in the Bible today because Paul didn't let what he could not do stop him from doing what he could do.

I pray that the Church will learn this important lesson in this very interesting season and embrace movement more than ever before. It's when we are moving with God and His plan that the world gets turned upside down for His glory (Acts 17:6). Let's choose to keep moving with God.

CONCLUSION

Will You Move?

Since you picked up this book, Earth is a little further along its orbit around the sun. Life is a bit different. You've met new people, had new experiences, and continued on the course that you've been on for the past year, two years, or more. The question isn't: Will you move? The question is: Will you move with God?

Will you dare to be faithful like Caleb, holding fast to God's promises, even if it takes decades to see them come true and you lose people along the way? Will you be willing, if God asks, to lead like Joshua, trusting that God will guide you when you don't know the way?

Moving with God requires strength. It requires you to be dissatisfied with the status quo, to embrace obstacles, and to be flexible in what God has for you. You will be different from those around you, and others may see you as crazy, but that's okay because God's approval is all you need.

God is with you, so take courage and move with Him! The journey starts now.

About the Author

Tim Hatch is the pastor of Waters Church, a multi-site and international congregation originating in New England, and the host of *The Deep End* podcast, where he teaches through Scripture verse by verse. He is married to Cheryl, and together they have three children—Alivia, Connor, and Jake. Tim earned his master's in theology from Knox Theological Seminary in 2015 and is currently enrolled in a Doctor of Ministry program. His passion is for the Church to live up to her calling in this generation, seeking to share the gospel and to pass on gospel-centered leadership to future generations.

About Sermon To Book

SermonToBook.com began with a simple belief: that sermons should be touching lives, *not* collecting dust. That's why we turn sermons into high-quality books that are accessible to people all over the globe.

Turning your sermon series into a book exposes more people to God's Word, better equips you for counseling, accelerates future sermon prep, adds credibility to your ministry, and even helps make ends meet during tight times.

John 21:25 tells us that the world itself couldn't contain the books that would be written about the work of Jesus Christ. Our mission is to try anyway. Because in heaven, there will no longer be a need for sermons or books. Our time is now.

If God so leads you, we'd love to work with you on your sermon or sermon series.

Visit www.sermontobook.com to learn more.

REFERENCES

Notes

[1] Herman, Rhett. "How Fast Is the Earth Moving?" Scientific American. October 26, 1998. https://www.scientific american.com/article/how-fast-is-the-earth-mov/.

[2] Williams, Matt. "What Is the Speed of Light?" Universe Today. September 1, 2016. https://www.universetoday.com/ 38040/speed-of-light-2/.

[3] McAdie, Alexander. *A Cloud Atlas*. Rand, McNally, 1923.

[4] National Ocean and Atmospheric Administration. "How Much Water Is in the Ocean?" National Ocean Service. https://oceanservice.noaa.gov/facts/oceanwater.html.

[5] "Plate Tectonics." *National Geographic*. https://www.nationalgeographic.com/science/earth/the-dynamic-earth/plate-tectonics/.

[6] "Body Basics: Heart and Circulatory System." Rady Children's Hospital – San Diego. https://www.rchsd.org/health-articles/heart-and-circulatory-system/.

[7] Frieberg, Kevin, and Jackie Frieberg. "The Belichick-Brady Way: 10 Lessons from the Patriots About the Art of Execution." Forbes. February 4, 2019. https://www.forbes.com/sites/kevinandjackiefreiberg/2019/02/04/the-belichick-brady-way-10-lessons-from-the-patriots-about-the-art-of-execution/#4bea33074c68.

[8] Edgar, William. "The Creation Mandate." The Gospel Coalition. https://www.thegospelcoalition.org/essay/the-creation-mandate/.

[9] Rowe, Mike. "Entrepreneuer: Don't Pursue Your Passion. Chase Opportunity." Mike Rowe (website). April 10, 2015. https://mikerowe.com/2015/04/entrepreneur-dont-pursue-your-passion-chase-opportunity/.

[10] Lewis, C. S. *The Weight of Glory*. HarperOne, 2009.

[11] Lawless, George P. "Saint Augustine: From Doubt to Certainty." Augustinian Vocations. July 17, 2015. https://augustinianvocations.org/blog-archive/2015/7/17/7rq2zq8wendiwe57i5zk9kg7tcu99q.

[12] Augustine. *Confessions* 1.1.5. In The Holy See. http://www.vatican.va/spirit/documents/spirit_20020821_agostino_en.html.

[13] Sacks, Jonathan. *Lessons in Leadership: A Weekly Reading of the Jewish Bible.* Maggid Books, 2015.

[14] Handey, Jack. *Fuzzy Memories.* Andrews McMeel Publishing, 1996.

[15] Stafford, Tom. "Psychology: Why Bad News Dominates the Headlines." BBC Future. July 29, 2014. https://www.bbc.com/future/article/20140728-why-is-all-the-news-bad.

[16] Longman, Tremper, III, and Raymond B. Dillard. *Introduction to the Old Testament.* Second edition. Zondervan Academic, 2009.

[17] Strong, James. "H1954: *Howsheah.*" *A Concise Dictionary of the Words in the Greek Testament and the Hebrew Bible.* Faithlife, 2020.

[18] Strong, James. "H3091: *Jehoshua.*" *A Concise Dictionary of the Words in the Greek Testament and the Hebrew Bible.* Faithlife, 2020.

[19] *Merriam-Webster*, "encourage." https://www.merriam-webster.com/dictionary/encourage.

[20] Anspaugh, David, dir. *Rudy.* TriStar, 1993.

[21] Christie, Vance. *Timeless Stories: God's Incredible Work in the Lives of Inspiring Christians.* Christian Focus Pulications, 2010.

[22] *Merriam-Webster*, "taunt." https://www.merriam-webster.com/dictionary/taunt.

[23] Strong, James. "H3091: *Jehoshua.*" *A Concise Dictionary of the Words in the Greek Testament and the Hebrew Bible.* Faithlife, 2020.

[24] Strong, James. "H3611: *Keleb.*" *A Concise Dictionary of the Words in the Greek Testament and the Hebrew Bible.* Faithlife, 2020.

[25] Strong, James. "H7497: *Raphah.*" *A Concise Dictionary of the Words in the Greek Testament and the Hebrew Bible.* Faithlife, 2020.

Made in the USA
Middletown, DE
13 March 2021